Ponderings

of a

Pedaling Pastor

DENNIS WHITMORE

InspiringVoices®

Scripture taken from the New King James Version. Copyright © 1979, 1980, 1982 by Thomas Nelson, Inc. Used by permission. All rights reserved.

Inspiring Voices books may be ordered through booksellers or by contacting:

Inspiring Voices
1663 Liberty Drive
Bloomington, IN 47403
www.inspiringvoices.com
1 (866) 697-5313

Because of the dynamic nature of the Internet, any web addresses or links contained in this book may have changed since publication and may no longer be valid. The views expressed in this work are solely those of the author and do not necessarily reflect the views of the publisher, and the publisher hereby disclaims any responsibility for them.

Any people depicted in stock imagery provided by Thinkstock are models, and such images are being used for illustrative purposes only.
Certain stock imagery © Thinkstock.

ISBN: 978-1-4624-1145-0 (sc)
ISBN: 978-1-4624-1146-7 (e)

Library of Congress Control Number: 2015911130

Print information available on the last page.

Inspiring Voices rev. date: 8/3/2015

Contents

Points to Ponder vii

1. Wake Up and Smell the Road Kill 1
2. Things Are Not Always as They Seem 3
3. Face up to Lack of Motivation 5
4. Underneath Are the Everlasting Arms 9
5. Lost for the Moment? Enjoy It 13
6. If You're Lost (or Not), Find True North 17
7. Frittering away the Time? 21
8. Wonders within Walking Distance 25
9. Thinking about the Great Hand on the Little Things 27
10. God-Incidences—Blessings in the Making 29
11. What's Love Got to Do with It? 33
12. Defining Our Heroes 37
13. Chance Encounters? 41
14. The Used-to-Bes and the Gonna-Bes 45
15. Training on Loving Life 49
16. God Understands 53
17. Run through Your Agony 57
18. The Letter from Home 61
19. Trophies and Their Stories 63
20. Ponderings of the Pedaling Pastor 67
21. Truth Really Can Be Stranger than Fiction and More Reliable 95
22. The Most Important Point to Ponder 99

About the Author 103

Points to Ponder

Random thoughts on things both great and small flow through our minds daily. Sometimes they distract us into a daydream; other times we may just reflect on the deeper meaning of the mundane, the redeeming qualities of the routine. Life goes on and on. Our hours and days flow by like a river. We forget much more than we remember, and what we do recall is usually a moment in time that packed an insight or taught a lesson. Perhaps it became a turning point in how we perceive life—even how we choose to live it.

Suppose you take one of those moments and examine it through the lens of Scripture. *Points to Ponder* are just that—moments in the course of life that invite reflection and thought from a biblical perspective.

Most of these points came during my morning devotional time. I read through the Bible, Genesis to Revelation, from January to December. Along the way, I pick up things that jump up and seem to say, "Hold up … look at that again." Other times, in the course of living my life, being a husband and father, dealing with people, or just observing the world, I ponder what I encounter. Sometimes I ponder it on paper, not knowing what conclusion I'll arrive at in the end.

I dedicate all of these to my high school guidance counselor, who once exclaimed to me, "*You have absolutely no writing talent whatsoever!*" She taught me one of the most valuable lessons of life. When being judged, whether one is being written up or written off: *consider the source.* Then do what's right.

Wake Up and Smell the Road Kill

One highlight of my summer is my annual bike trip, usually into Virginia. It is my time with God. As I ride alone for many hours, I can pray and reflect. My prayer time is mostly just quiet listening as He brings insights and lessons to my mind.

Along the road, of course, I see (and smell) road kill. It is close on a bike, and it takes a bit more time to get past it. It can be very distracting. But as I reflect on all the beauty of God's creation, the gift of good health that He's given me, and the sense of His protective presence along the way, I am able to move beyond the unpleasant things along the road.

How about you? Are you able to move beyond the unpleasant things along the road? The longer we allow ourselves to be distracted by dwelling on these things, the less interested we will be in the flowers of life. Consider the thoughts that occupy your mind and guide your perspective on things. Are you responding with wonder and gratitude to the flowers?

As the apostle Paul sat in a cold, smelly, awful prison, notice the focus of his mind as he wrote to the church in Philippi:

> Be anxious for nothing, but in everything by prayer and supplication, with thanksgiving, let your requests be made known to God. (Philippians 4:6)

In other words, talk to God. Keep the line open, listening for His still, small voice. With a thankful, appreciative attitude, turn to God and open your heart. Let your heavenly Father know how you feel and what you need, "And the peace of God which surpasses all understanding, will guard your hearts and minds through Christ Jesus" (v. 7).

Do not be distracted by the dead things, the unpleasant sights and awful smells you will encounter on the road of daily life. But as Paul reminds us, from within the midst of ugly sights and offensive smells,

> Whatever things are pure, whatever things are lovely, whatever things are of good report, if there is any virtue and if there is anything praiseworthy meditate on these things. The things which you learned and received and saw in me, these do, and the God of peace will be with you. (vss. 8–9)

As someone once said, it is not what happens to us in life, it is what we do with what happens to us. In any matter, what we choose to do begins with the perspective we choose to take. So focus your mind on the goodness of God, and as the Scripture assures us, "My God shall supply all your needs according to His riches in glory by Christ Jesus" (v. 19).

Things Are Not Always as They Seem

Years ago I was cycling home on a familiar road. It consisted of a series of roller coaster-type hills; up, then down, then up again. It was raining and cold as I turned onto that road to begin taking on the first of the several hills. As I puffed up the grade, I looked through the raindrops to the yellow diamond-shaped road sign. It said, "Steep hills ahead." At least that's what I saw.

I shook my head in disbelief, and sure enough, it did not say anything like that. I had already been over a steep mountain some miles ago. The rains came. I had seventy miles to go. Hard work and several hours of pedaling were ahead of me. And so my mind processed all of that and projected onto the warning sign a message that was not there.

When we're going through a hard time, on a long stretch of life's road, our minds can project into the situation negative thoughts, and even prophecies of our imminent doom. How often do you make a hard situation even harder because you listen to what seems to be, rather than what is?

In Lamentations 3, in the midst of a destroyed Jerusalem, the prophet Jeremiah says, "Through the Lord's mercies, we are not consumed because His compassions fail not. They are new every morning. Great is Your faithfulness." And Paul writes from a cold jail cell in Philippians 4:13, "I can do all things through Christ who strengthens me."

Whatever life *seems* to be, remember—God is. Great is His faithfulness.

Face up to Lack of Motivation

I don't want to exercise.

I feel unmotivated for sometimes a month or more to get to the gym, ride the bike, lift the weights. Yet for thirty years I have worked out consistently, three to four days per week. Many a morning I'll be riding the cycle in the spin class (an aerobic bicycling class that uses stationary bikes), and the thought will come: *I could leave now.* Some days, I am just not in the mood to push myself. Yet I do.

How many of us confuse motivation with ability? In other words, if I really don't *feel* like doing something—even the thought of it is painful—that means I can't do it. If I'm unwilling, therefore I am unable. That, of course, is self-deception; a lie that caters to one's lazy side.

One morning, the spin instructor was preparing us for the all-terrain ride we were to embark upon for forty-five minutes. She gave us a point to ponder: "When things get uncomfortable, growth happens."

Now there's a thought. Has anything worth having or achieving come to us without struggle or hard work? It was a challenging phrase. How many of us are motivated to enter the zone of uncomfortable at full throttle? And then once you've crossed the threshold (where you're thinking, *I'm not liking this.*), you plow through with dedicated persistence. If you have ever done that, you know from past experience that once you're on the other side of that zone, something good awaits—not a mere trophy or a promotion necessarily but a discovery about yourself. Many people don't stick with the tough stuff long enough to find out.

In these thirty years of working out, I have moved from Maryland to North Carolina and back, changed careers, gone to seminary, got married and had two children, and dealt with many life-altering changes.

Yet, through all of them and the convenient excuses they provided me for quitting exercise, I only missed one week of workouts. And that was because a leg infection had me laid up.

I am healthy today, but for a number of months, I have lacked motivation to keep to my exercise routine. I have struggled with these seasons of sluggishness before—more times than I can count. But feeling motivated is not a qualification for compelling motivation. My brain is capable of ordering one leg and then the other to go. And they will comply.

But how does one get motivated or stay motivated to do something that one lacks the internal motivation to do? For thirty years I have been able to consistently push myself to do my workouts whether I felt like it or not. Really, what *difference does it make* whether I feel like doing it or not?

Here's the key I have discovered: thanksgiving. Or to expand it: thankfulness, praise and worship, gratitude. The lesson has become over time standard equipment in my soul.

> Rejoice always, pray without ceasing, in everything give thanks; for this is the will of God in Christ Jesus for you. (1 Thessalonians 5:16–18)

This instruction is standard in that when I am doing a class or an exercise that I do not feel in the mood to do, a phrase comes forth from my heart to my lips: "Thank You, Lord" or "Thank You, Father." When I complete a set of exercises, I sometimes say, "Praise God!" Why? Because I can do what I just did. Life and all of its benefits are gifts. And these gifts are special blessings that should be appreciated and cared for.

I began working out thirty years ago because I got a job at a health club. I had to learn about exercise. Many of the sales staff did not work out, but I felt duty-bound to study and use the product we were selling. It took me two years to figure out a routine that worked for me. In those early years, it was tough to stick with it. But I had to find a way, because I was preaching to clients that lifestyle management was a necessity.

I know how hard it is to get started, and then to stay with it. I am struggling with it now. But, how you *feel*—whether you like it or not—is irrelevant. Your life on earth is a stewardship. Many of the diseases that burden us are preventable. One of the biggest health problems in our country is obesity. This does not have to be.

Change begins with one's attitude. From a prison Paul tells us:

> Be anxious for nothing, but in everything by prayer and supplication, with thanksgiving, let your requests be made known to God. (Philippians 4:6)

In other words, talk to God about it. Express your needs. And with a thankful attitude, get going.

Underneath Are the Everlasting Arms

We have a few patches of protruding rocks on our property. When she was four years old, our daughter, Joanna, would go to each one and conquer the summit—climbing, twisting, and reaching her little arms and legs, determined to make her goal. As her dad, of course, I'm looking at the slippery flat sides, the sharp edges, and the length of the drop from the top to the grass below. Potential concussions, broken bones, and other possible disasters flash through my mind as I keep a firm hand extended beneath her but just beyond touching her. That's the rule; I'm not supposed to help.

The trees she liked to climb were even more frightening. She'd go much higher, sometimes just beyond my reach. I tried to remember how my dad let me do goofy stuff and risk my life. "How else are you gonna learn?" he would say. The question I ask now, reflecting back on his wisdom, is this: After I awake from the coma, would I remember what I learned?

I take long cycling trips for a week every summer, largely because the first time was Dad's idea. I was seventeen, had a ten-speed bike, and often took rides from our home in Baltimore out to the county and back. Why not go a little farther?

Over Labor Day weekend, the family was going camping near Gettysburg. Dad suggested (without checking with my mother) that I ride my bike from home to the campground after I finished doing my newspaper route. I was on my way. Many of the roads were still rural and traffic was not so bad—but my mother probably aged ten years overnight waiting for me to arrive safely.

It took all night. I had to repair my rear wheel, dragging the bike into a cornfield with a flashlight. Later I was chased by dogs. My bike drove like a truck, having over packed the panniers ("saddle bags"); plus everything with wheels was heavy in the 1970s—the wide cars and the steel-frame bicycles.

It was an adventure. I arrived by 10:00 a.m. the next morning. I had survived the night, and that meant my father would survive the rest of the day; the wrath of Mom had subsided at the sight of her son still intact.

I often thought through that long night of climbing hills and slowly plodding along. What was my father thinking? With sweat pouring down my face that summer night, I jokingly grunted to myself: "He either really trusts me or he's trying to get me killed." There was just a wisdom in my dad about how much he could trust me—how far he could push me, or let the latest challenge do it. As a boy, he didn't have a dad around. He and his older sister and three brothers weathered some tough times together. Life is rough, but how else are you going to learn? Learn what? What you can do, what you should—and should not—do, and what it means to take a risk.

That night in 1977, there were no cell phones. Only an occasional pay phone appeared along my route. Who could I call? He had a map, and he knew my route. He gave me time. And he waited—just far enough away, but close enough if he had to come. So much of that first trip on my bike was about a son taking a risk on his own because his dad believed he could do it.

In 2006, I rode my bike to Laurel, Mississippi—1,071 miles over twelve days. But that trip had its beginning almost thirty years earlier because Dad was waiting in Gettysburg. It was his idea for me to try it.

> The calling of our heavenly Father is like that too. To a teenager named Jeremiah, He said, "Before I formed you in the womb I knew you" (Jeremiah 1:5 NKJV).

It stands to reason He knows each one of us just as well. We're custom-built, by hand. And for what purpose, what grand plan does He envision for the woman or the man He has made of you? To discover that, to explore it, to embrace it, to believe it, to finally devote your life to it, it will begin with a risk. Climbing that rock. Reaching a little higher for that branch. Taking that journey that He has inspired in your heart to try. How cool is that?

One day as Joanna climbed, she reached her foot toward a branch. I warned her not to do it. I could see it was weak. She did, and I moved my hand toward her. Her weight went on to that branch, and it snapped. She fell out of the tree. My waiting hand caught her. I believe it is like that with our heavenly Father. Along the way we will step too far, put our full weight on the wrong support, or take a shot and miss. But He is faithful and is watching and waiting. He knows our potential.

> The eternal God is your refuge and underneath are the everlasting arms. (Deuteronomy 33:27a)

Lost for the Moment? Enjoy It

It was our first bike ride of the spring season. A beautiful spring day. Elizabeth (eleven) took the lead, Joanna (six) followed, and then I fell in behind. "Let's explore that road we didn't follow to the end last year," Elizabeth said. It was Gift Road, which starts as asphalt then transitions to dirt and protruding rock. Joanna, being new to the two-wheeled bike, bounced to a stop on the downhill. She fell over but recovered well. Elizabeth, meanwhile, followed the road to the end. When Joanna and I arrived, walking our bikes, I pointed to the now visible Potomac—we were at the C & O Canal towpath. For them, a new discovery!

Having ridden bicycles over many years, I knew their little legs only had so many miles of power in them. But they were up for it, so we went left. On and on we rode the path. I knew we were getting farther and farther away from home. Plus, if there was no other access point, we would have to go to Williamsport before we could turn toward home. That would be six miles, in addition to whatever we were racking up on the way. Fortunately, they did not realize this.

They were good sports about it—until the swarm of gnats met us. Big ones, too. We had to stop and brush them off our legs and arms.

Then the whining began: "I want to go home."

After about a mile, there was a dirt path across a field and leading to blacktop road. I sent Elizabeth to scout it out. There were no signs or familiar landmarks. I remembered back when I got lost for the first time. I was about Elizabeth's age and size—and riding the gold bicycle she now rides. (It had been my first bike, which my parents gave me for Christmas over forty years ago.)

So I proudly declared, "Hey ... we're lost!" There was a moment of stunned silence, so I added, "Isn't this great!" The wise older child inquired, of course, as to why this was a good thing. I pointed to her bike and said, "That bike and I did this a lot ... It's an adventure." I looked at my watch and said, "We've got about three hours before sunset to find our way home ... Yay!" I figured we were on Bottom Road, but I wanted to enjoy the uncertainty of it all. Though I had years of experience and fairly good discernment for figuring out where I was, I wanted to see this time through their eyes. It was a totally new experience—a strange place with no clue on how to get home or how long it would take to get there.

It's often the "not knowing" that throws us into a panic. Can you recall moments in your life's journey when you were at a point that had no familiar landmarks? How would you get out of that fix? How long would it take? Which way should you turn?

The whining to go home transitioned to an occasionally mentioned request. The girls seemed to follow my cue and took on the challenge. Elizabeth rode on out of sight; then she'd wait for Joanna and me to catch up. I observed the girls' behavior during this wilderness experience. Elizabeth would go on and explore, then report what she saw. Joanna, who started out from home unable to mount her bike without me holding it steady, now was saying, "I can do it." On one long hill, after we'd stopped, she got on her bike and took to climbing it the rest of the way.

In the two hours since we had left home, both girls had adapted to the journey and its demands. Joanna, in just one afternoon, became a much more competent and assertive cyclist. How could they do that?

It's the same way you and I do it when we're traveling through life's unfamiliar, challenging terrain. They did not dwell on all the dangers and risks and things that could paralyze them with fear. They trusted their dad.

I had declared it an adventure—so it became just that. If I had said we were in trouble, they would have felt that. I bore the burden of the unknown *for them*. All they had to do was follow my directions and ride well.

Have you entered a fearful time—a place with no familiar landmarks? If you will realize that your heavenly Father is with you on this trip, you can let Him bear the burden of the unanswered questions. In His company, life is a series of adventures.

> Fear not, for I am with you; be not dismayed, for I am your God. I will strengthen you, yes, I will help you. I will uphold you with My righteous right hand. (Isaiah 41:10)

If You're Lost (or Not),
Find True North

I carry a compass when I take long bicycle rides. Several years ago, I'd ridden along some winding country road that brought me to a three-pronged fork—three options that went into three different directions. Since it was high noon, I could not tell which direction any of them would take me. With compass in hand, I located true north, thereby orienting myself and the options before me. I could choose a path.

The thing about choosing a path is that you have to reject the other options. Sometimes you know full well which way not to go. But as you leave behind those other possibilities, sometimes you reflect on what might have been. You'll never really know, because that road is now closed. And at times you'll wonder (no matter how convinced you still are): Did I do the right thing? What might have happened if ...?

Someone has said that a person is the sum total of all the decisions (choices) he or she has made in life. You can look back at the path you have taken and can see key turning points. Some were poor judgment calls; others were wisely considered and well-timed. Sometimes (perhaps most of the time) you have made decisions without really thinking through the consequences or even realizing there would be consequences. And sometimes, you realize in retrospect that it was a relatively minor decision that put you on the major highway that became the journey you've been living: your life.

My first real job as a college student was in a restaurant. It was there that I met the one whom I would marry. After graduation in 1983, with unemployment being so high and jobs scarce, I grabbed the first job I could get: health club sales. That job became my career and taught me valuable self-care and self-discipline techniques. Though I never liked being in sales, I had the best training. This helped me discover my abilities as a teacher and communicator (useful in pastoral care). I came to understand the spiritual development of a person by working with the physical development and fitness of people.

Everything I was doing would lead me to something else. One place served as the stepping stone to the next place, sometimes without me knowing there was a next place up ahead.

The old saying goes, "One door closes, another door opens." That may offer some consolation after an unexpected loss. But I have wondered: Does it always happen in *that order*? Does a door have to close on one thing before the door opens to the next thing? Is there sometimes a delay in between? Suppose a door has opened before you but the one that needs to close is still open. Do you leave before you go—or do you go before you leave?

It helps to have a reliable moral compass, one that readily shows you where you are even if every other indicator around will not. If you know where true north is, then every other option and opportunity sits before you in a discernible position. Meaning what?

It is never clear which option is perfect, or even what each outcome will be, but if you are clear about your own position, you can place the options in proper perspective. For instance, I did not want to work in a restaurant. But my moral compass tells me that your name goes on the work you do. Lousy work equals a lousy name. The axiom made a dull job more fun and gave me a solid reference for future jobs.

Likewise, I never wanted to be in sales, yet for about ten years—a full *decade*—I was in sales jobs. I kept reading and listening to tapes and learning from others how to be better at this work I did not like. Again, the moral compass pointed me to true north. Scripture says it well:

> Whatever your hand finds to do, do it with all your might.
> (Ecclesiastes 9:10)

> And whatever you do, do it heartily, as to the Lord and not to men, knowing that from the Lord you will receive the reward of the inheritance; for you serve the Lord Christ.
> (Colossians 3:23–24)

As I worked hard, even in jobs I did not like, I found that it developed my character and trained me in perseverance. When I finally achieved a level of security, decent income, and good benefits, I was able to see the trap these things can set.

Options arose. The risks meant leaving these things I had worked hard for. Again I pulled out the compass and saw that true north was not in those other directions; it is the position from which I can properly see those directions and the paths toward which they point.

Every path we take leads to a crossroads eventually. Options present themselves. Denying some to pursue others is necessary. Even doing nothing is a choice. But if you don't regularly check your compass for true north, you may find yourself lost along the way. You may be on a path that *feels wrong* but you don't know why. Or you may mistakenly make a wrong turn because you're flying by the seat of your pants instead of pulling out the compass from your pants' pocket.

Jesus said, "Seek first the Kingdom of God" (Matthew 6:33), the rule and standard of God. When you decide to do that, then open your Bible and your heart; you will find *your* true north.

Frittering away the Time?

What have you been missing because you have no time to just think? Actually, we all have the time, we just misappropriate it.

I took a five-day bicycling trip from my Clear Spring, Maryland, home to Charlottesville, Virginia, and back. I spent many hours pedaling through beautiful country and did a lot of thinking. Yet by day's end, I had failed to write down a lot of my thoughts. As I rode, I would drift from one topic to another without deeply reflecting on some of the interesting things my ride time was affording me to consider.

At the hotel each night, I would watch television to catch the news. I found it rather addictive though I am not one to watch TV at home. "Breaking News" was often the title of the day as a program would commence. Yet the actual news was that there was no news. I watched three programs in a row, each covering the same issue. The same points and counter-points were made—sometimes with the same guest commentators. By evening's end, I had no more information from those hours of broadcasts than I'd normally get in a five-minute radio news summary. I wasted huge amounts of time to stimulate my mind with information that had little substantive value. Yet earlier that day, my own mind in quiet reflection in the saddle gave me a wide range of information. Just mulling over day-to-day observations was stimulating insights that, if taken time to explore, would deepen my understanding of life, the world around me, God, and myself.

I pondered. Why do I resist the deeper, richer experiences and choose hours of pointless television programming? The purpose of these things is to compel viewers to stay in front of the box and watch the commercials. Pure manipulation—yet it works. Why is that so?

Since I had time to spend hours just thinking, pondering, reading, and writing, it was obvious that I was *choosing* a compelling distraction. I was filling hours with television. I determined that it takes strength of will to sit still and really think for a length of time. A lot of us say we would like to "Just have time to think," as if someone steals our time away. I submit that we fritter our time away, as John Wesley used to say. We take the path of least resistance and allow the box to do our thinking for us.

Count the number of hours per day you put into watching TV. By the end of the seven-day week, you may find you've spent the equivalent of one full twenty-four-hour day at an activity that has yielded you precisely *what*?

Carrying this point further, why do people have more than one television? Why is it often in the center of the home? Why must the bedroom have one? Really ... *Why?*

What real, live person in your actual day-to-day life has as many hours of your attention as your TV does?

There was a college fund commercial years ago that made a good point: "A mind is a terrible thing to waste." Kind of ironic that it was a television commercial.

Moses offers a worthy prayer:

> So teach us to number our days, that we may gain a heart of wisdom. (Psalm 90:12)

We do need to value our days, to determine the eternal significance of how we are investing the time—or just frittering it away. One can always make more money, but no one can make more time. Even God does not remake a day. They come and they go. And then one day, they are gone. Time's up.

I am not picking on television, per se. I am reflecting on a behavioral choice we often make without considering what we are giving up by making it. How well are we counting the days, exercising our minds, and growing in wisdom?

I baptized a new believer on a late summer day. A month later, I found him crying in his hospital bed. The cancer was terminal. He cried, not because he would soon be dead, but because for decades he had failed to really live. His new relationship with the Lord had opened his eyes to it all. But his time was up.

How well do we invest our time? Do we ever stop and think? Do we ever stop to *just think*?

Wonders within Walking Distance

When I lived in Baltimore, I loved to take my annual summer bicycle trip to my parents' trailer at the River Bend Park near Falling Waters, West Virginia. I'd stay for a week, making day trips into Hagerstown, Maryland. Grabbing a paper and a coffee, I'd pedal down to City Park and enjoy the beauty of a quiet morning among the ducks there. I have always loved the City Park; it was a highlight of my summer to get out of Baltimore to come west and hang out in the Hub City.

Now we live in Clear Spring, ten miles away instead of ninety. Yet I rarely ride to the park. It's always nearby and available to me if I want to go. But I don't do it.

I grew up in South Baltimore, only one mile from Fort McHenry, home of "The Star-Spangled Banner." I recall seeing RVs in the parking lot there from as far away as Nevada. *That cost a small fortune for that family to come here,* I thought to myself. I was blessed to be able to visit anytime I wanted, for free. But I rarely did.

My boyhood home was walking distance from Harbor Place, the National Aquarium, the Constellation, and many other tourist sites. During my senior year at Southern High School, I went across the street to Federal Hill and watched this now-famous area being built. Yet while I lived there, I didn't think much about what we had available to us, with no need for a parking space.

While living in Laurel, Maryland, a few years ago, I could have ridden my bike to the National Mall, the Lincoln Memorial, and all over our beautiful Capitol in about an hour. But I rarely made the trip. It was always there if I wanted to go; I just never got around to it.

Isn't it interesting that we go to such great expense and effort to get to a special place? But the treasures nearest to us we tend to overlook.

I guess we figure it will always be there to suit our convenience. Is that what we mean by "familiarity breeds contempt"? Do you get so used to having blessings at your disposal that you forget how blessed you are?

As Moses prepared the Israelites to leave their wilderness camp and take possession of the Promised Land, he reminded them of how blessed they were. Despite our nation's problems, as we reflect on the sacrifices of so many to win and to preserve our freedoms, Moses could just as well be speaking to us.

> For what great nation is there that has God so near it, as the Lord our God is to us, for whatever reason we may call upon Him? And what great nation is there that has such statutes and righteous judgments as are in all this law which I set before you this day? Only take heed to yourself, and diligently keep yourself, lest you forget the things your eyes have seen, and lest they depart from your heart all the days of your life. And teach them to your children and your grandchildren. (Deuteronomy 4:7–9)

A relationship with the God who created you—what a blessing to have so near at hand. Yet He is so familiar and conveniently close that we fail to make time to connect with Him. We'll go to great lengths and great expense to find rest or some such thing that we think will satisfy. We build our homes and then spend all kinds of money to get away from them. Sometimes it's good to just stay home and look around. And if you'll *make* time (because you'll never *find* it) to see what you're looking at, you may discover treasures that have been waiting to be found.

The apostle Paul said it well, that God made each of us to dwell in a certain place in the world at a certain time in history.

> So that they should seek the Lord in the hope that they might grope for Him and find Him, though He is not far from each one of us. (Acts 17:27)

When you realize that you are searching for something, slow down and pay attention. You may be looking at the very thing you've been failing to see—and appreciate. The best things in life are within walking distance if you are walking with the Lord.

Thinking about the
Great Hand on the Little Things

While bicycling on a rural road, I witnessed a squirrel being struck by a car. Unfortunately the poor creature was not killed instantly. It lay helpless in the road gasping for air and in pain, barely moving. As I gently placed his warm little body in a box in an attempt to put him in a safe place, my eyes filled up. I watched him, feeling guilty that I could do nothing to ease the pain or to provide healing. I thought about the One from whom this little life had come. I thought about how tragically dangerous this world is for the innocents—the small animals of the wild as well as the children in our communities. Both can be so ignorant of the hazards of life.

Watching a small animal die brought so many incredibly diverse thoughts to my mind—unrelated yet profound truths that would otherwise never come up. This little life stopped me for a half hour, and it has forever affected me. Consider this profound truth.

> I said in my heart, "Concerning the condition of the sons of men, God tests them, that they may see that they themselves are like animals." For what happens to the sons of men also happens to animals; one thing befalls them: as one dies, so dies the other. Surely, they all have one breath; man has no advantage over animals, for all is vanity. All go to one place: all are from the dust, and all return to dust. (Ecclesiastes 3:18–20)

On the physical level, our bodies come and go, live and die, just as those of the animals. But Scripture says that we are made in the image of God (Genesis 1:26–27). Our lives are more than our bodies.

Isn't it interesting how much attention we devote to our physical existence? Our wants become needs. Desires for fleeting pleasures, perceived security, and whatever constitutes for us "the American Dream" become vain obsessions. Life is so much more. It's so sacred, yet quietly so. You really don't appreciate this until you deal with death.

As I rode away from that scene, I was so aware of the presence of life: trees, flowers, the cattle and horses in the fields, the mountain up ahead. The source of it all is He who gives the breath of life and takes it away. Maybe the Lord wanted me at that intersection that day so He could teach me something profound, which is often revealed in the simple.

My encounter with this squirrel happened years ago, before I was a pastor, before the first of the 150-plus funerals I have conducted.

How else could I have so deeply appreciated what I had seen? The awesome God in whom we believe is involved in all life. I am so thankful for all I know of our Lord and for all He is about to teach me as I live day by day. I hope that you will take time this day to get to know better the One from whom all life comes!

> Praise the LORD! Oh, give thanks to the LORD, for He is good! For His mercy endures forever. Who can utter the mighty acts of the LORD? Who can declare all His praise? (Psalm 106:1–2)

God-Incidences—Blessings
in the Making

I look for *God-incidences*. A lot of people call them coincidences, but that's probably because they're not paying attention. Often they happen while you're on the way to do one thing, then this other thing occurs at just the right time. Your whole day can be redirected by one interruption. On a recent bicycle tour, this happened to me.

Every spring I ride in the MS (multiple sclerosis) Bike Tour. The year that it was in Chestertown, on Maryland's eastern shore, I was to go to a prayer conference in Seaford, Delaware (about sixty miles), the next day. With rain in the forecast, I decided to leave the MS Tour Sunday route and ride my bike toward Seaford, planning to layover in Denton, as the conference would begin late on Monday.

Nature's call compelled me to stop at a convenience store outside Greensboro. It was seven miles to Denton, but the situation was a bit urgent, so I asked a man coming out the door if there was a restroom. He said he had a hotel down the street and welcomed me to follow him there.

It was the Riverside Inn, a century-old two-story hotel that overlooks the Choptank River. Doug, the owner, warmly welcomed me to relax awhile in the upstairs, enclosed porch. With windows all around and a cool breeze blowing through, he offered refreshments and all the time I wanted, to just hang out.

Doug and his wife have refurbished this fine old place, a mixture of late nineteenth–century architectural style mixed with modern features our spoiled generation has come to expect. Discovering that I was a pastor, he introduced me to a family friend who came by to help around the place.

Estelle, having heard that a "minister on his bike" had dropped by, brought her grandmother's King James Bible and came to meet me. She loves the Lord, loves to pray and do Bible study. My original plan after finding those necessary facilities was to find a church to attend on the way to Denton; however, it turned out that I would have church right there with Estelle.

We did what Jesus told the very first Christians to do—"be witnesses of Me" (Acts 1:8): Tell your story of what you've heard and seen Me do. We walked through several Scripture passages, dealing with some concerns and questions she'd been burdened with for some time. This was a God-incident. My immediate needs had brought me there. Her need for scriptural guidance was answered by the "coincidence" of my well-timed arrival.

I stayed at Doug's hotel that night, instead of going on to Denton. He and his wife, Mary, were so hospitable (and they needed the business more than the Best Western in Denton).

Estelle baked an angel food cake with blue icing—"for blue skies." It was sort of a confectionary prayer (if you bake it, so it will be). It was a thank-you gift to have with my coffee, which Doug brewed and brought over the following morning before I left.

How good it is to touch lives and to be touched by them. A series of small decisions led me to that little hotel that I did not even know existed. Nor did I know that Doug, Mary, and Estelle existed either. But by coincidence our paths crossed. A God-incident, in that such blessings do not happen by chance.

In an earlier time of my life, I might have missed this beautiful change of plans. I have always been a scheduled, get-it-done type person. I pace my bike trips so that my rest intervals are properly timed, I get the miles done, and I get to where I have to be in an efficient manner. But that day, I saw the potential for an adventure in blessing. I was looking for a restroom and found a cool hotel. I was looking for a church to attend, and I had church right there among new friends. I lingered in Greensboro far longer than I normally would have, and that was okay. Relationships take time. Estelle still stays in touch.

I believe that God puts us in the lives of others by plotting "intercept courses." God sees who's traveling in what direction. He knows who needs to meet *you* and when. You don't know enough of the big picture to see where you need to be, but He does. And "things happen." Sometimes it's just best to roll with it. It may be a *God-incident* in the making. An adventure in blessing for someone—possibly you—is being written by the Author of life.

> You comprehend my path and my lying down, and are acquainted with all my ways ... You have hedged me behind and before, and laid Your hand upon me. Such knowledge is too wonderful for me; it is high, I cannot attain it. (Psalm 139:3, 5–6)

What's Love Got to Do with It?

From my topical files, I pulled one entitled, "Love." Among the collection of clippings I have stored there, two columns fell out, side by side. One was from *People* magazine, "The End of the Road" (9/22/03); the other was "Muriel's Blessing," from *Christianity Today* (2/5/96). *Love* is perhaps the most misused term in our culture. From sappy and silly "love songs" to the "love scenes" (which are actually sex scenes) in movies and TV, our society seems confused. What does real love have to do with any of it? Especially when you take a vow before God to love and honor your spouse "till death do us part." These two articles, lying side by side before me, got me thinking. "For better or for worse" is a vow one should not make lightly.

"Muriel's Blessing," written by Dr. Robertson McQuilkin, was a follow up of a 1990 interview by *Christianity Today*. Both explored the "or worse" part of living out the marriage vows till death.

In the 1996 article, McQuilkin picks up in the seventeenth year of his wife's long journey with Alzheimer's disease. He had stepped down as president of what is today Columbia International University in South Carolina to provide full-time care to his wife, Muriel. As her condition deteriorated over the previous five years, he gained deeper insights into the mysteries of love and marriage.

In recalling a time when he was cleaning up one of Muriel's bathroom accidents, she was "helping." As he was trying to fend her off and clean simultaneously, Pastor Chuck Swindoll, booming from the radio, said, "Men! Are you at home? *Really* at home?" McQuilkin writes, "I smiled, 'Yeah, Chuck, I really am.' Do I ever wish I weren't?" His answer—no.

Alongside of McQuilkin's amazing account of sacrificial love for his wife, Muriel, I had the story of Lance Armstrong's marriage, "The End of the Road." At the time, he had won five of the eventual string of seven Tour de France victories; a rising star as an athlete and cancer survivor.

The summary statement at the front of this article: "Cycling champion Lance Armstrong reveals how his athletic success helped lead to a rare defeat: The unraveling of his five-year marriage."

Armstrong had beaten testicular cancer in 1997, was married to Kristen ("Kik") in 1998, and won his first Tour de France in 1999. In his first book, *It's Not about the Bike*, he described his amazing against-the-odds defeat of cancer, how he and Kik had met, and how they fought the disease together. He described how, together, they "rebuilt" him, thus enabling him to win perhaps the most grueling endurance race in the world. Endurance race—yes. That too is what marriage is; love is what keeps it going to the finish line.

"Love suffers long … endures … never fails" (1 Corinthians 13:4, 7d, 8a).

Armstrong credits cancer as being a great "gift" that taught him how to make pain work for him. In all seven Tour de France races, he surged ahead in the mountain-climb stages, coming out victorious at the end. He said he could push through the pain of those long climbs because of a well of deeper strength cancer had helped him to find.

Cancer did not beat him. The best athletes and toughest mountains in France could not defeat him. But success did. Armstrong said, "All I knew was that in trying to do everything, we'd forgotten to do the most important thing. We forgot to be married."

Then I reread "Muriel's Blessing," in which McQuilkin describes the pain he climbed through: the death of his eldest son, "my dearest (wife) slipping away," and his life's work "abandoned at its peak" so he could care for Muriel.

It was Valentine's Day, 1948, when Muriel had accepted his marriage proposal. On Valentine's Day eve, 1995, he read something about how the caregiver is the true victim of Alzheimer. He said he never felt like a victim. He loved her.

That night he bathed Muriel in bed, tucked her in, and kissed her goodnight, praying the Lord would keep her till morning.

The next morning I was peddling on my Exercycle at the foot of her bed and reminiscing about some of our happy lovers' day long gone while Muriel slowly emerged from sleep. Finally, she popped awake and, as she often does, smiled at me. Then, for the first time in months she spoke, calling out to me in a voice clear as a crystal chime, "Love … love … love." I jumped from my cycle and ran to embrace her. "Honey, you really do love me, don't you?" Holding me with her eyes and patting my back, she responded with the only words she could find to say yes: "I'm nice," she said. Those may prove to be the last words she ever spoke.

In his article, Armstrong concluded:

> People warn you that marriage is hard work, but you don't listen. You talk about the pretty bridesmaids' dresses, but you don't talk about what happens next; about how difficult it will be to stay, or to rebuild. What nobody tells you is that there will be more than just some hard days. There will be some hard weeks and perhaps even some hard years. In February I returned to Europe for training alone, and Kik stayed behind in Austin. We intended to bring the same dedication and discipline to counseling that we brought to the rest of our lives.

He said that their marriage had been a success because it produced "three great prizes," their children. But I wonder what he lost by not staying in the race.

I don't write this to judge Armstrong or venerate McQuilkin. It makes me think on this: "Love never fails" (1 Corinthians 13:8a).

What am *I* doing in my life and in my marriage with that truth?

Defining Our Heroes

Lance Armstrong's rise and fall as a sports hero also prompts me to consider what the essence of a true hero is. I recall that day in a bookstore when I picked up Lance Armstrong's then recently released book, *It's Not about the Bike*. I sat down and read the first three chapters, captivated by his story: being raised by a single mom, finding his love for cycling and his ability to win races, winning his struggle against cancer, and then taking on the Tour de France. I was especially inspired by how he would take on the grueling hill climbs in the Tour with tenacity. He described how cancer had taught him how to use pain rather than be hindered by it.

His later divorce from his wife, whom he described in the book with such love, shocked and disappointed me. She had been with him in the fight against his cancer. Subsequent articles and interviews seemed to describe how the lifestyle of a pro cyclist was the reason for the demise of their marriage. The long months of training, the random drug tests at any time of any day, which often interrupted family time, the long separations for events—these took their toll. Who can really know the details? But I began to think that maybe it *was* all about the bike after all.

Over the years, Armstrong vehemently denied charges that he was "doping." All seven Tour de France victories were accomplished without performance-enhancing drugs, he claimed. The French seemed to be out to get him, and many of us believed it.

But now, it has been proven true. Armstrong isn't even fighting it anymore. I guess, once you're a multimillionaire, who cares anymore what people say?

So then, maybe it really *was Not about the Bike*. But what was it all about? The mother of his children is no longer his wife; he's since moved on to other women and more children. The big, world-renowned racing events are over for him at this point. Plus, the seven Tour de France wins were all lies.

> All things come alike to all: One event happens to the righteous and the wicked; to the good, the clean, and the unclean; to him who sacrifices and him who does not sacrifice. As is the good, so is the sinner; he who takes an oath as he who fears an oath. This is an evil in all that is done under the sun: that one thing happens to all. (Ecclesiastes 9:2–3a)

That one thing is death. No amount of money or power can buy anyone out of that.

> Truly the hearts of the sons of men are full of evil; madness is in their hearts while they live, and after that they go to the dead. (3b)

There is a truth we seldom reflect upon: your name lives on even after your body has died. When you breathe your last, your name goes on a death certificate. Then it comes off of everything else. Only your name continues to be yours and over time, carries into future generations a summary of your character.

George Washington died over two hundred years ago, yet his name stands for character and integrity. On the other hand, you don't have to be a historian to know the name Benedict Arnold stands for traitor. I don't know any parents who name their baby boys Judas nowadays either.

It's interesting to consider the irony of having the news about Lance Armstrong's cheating on the same day a Pakistani girl's name is being heard around the world: Malala Yousufzai. At age fourteen, she dared to risk her life by speaking out against the Taliban. She dared to go to school, to fight for her right to an education (the Taliban opposes the education of girls). The cowards were so threatened by the little girl's boldness that they hunted her down and shot her and two of her friends on the way to school.

She could have died. She risked her body and her life for what is right. Even if she had died, she beat the Taliban by the strength of her character.

To have her name and Lance Armstrong's reported in the same paper on the same day is worth pondering. If there was ever a question as to whether character counts, a Pakistani girl answered it. And it doesn't matter whether Malala Yousufzai even knew how to ride a bike.

It is a fascinating thing to observe what people will give their lives to and how, in the end, the true measure of success is often not what one may have first thought.

Chance Encounters?

When I was a new pastor, I tried to get out and meet church members, particularly the shut-ins. I'd heard that one of our very elderly ladies was in the hospital so I went to meet her.

I went to her bed by the window, business card and Bible in hand. Her oxygen mask was hanging off her pale, thin face. As she looked up, I introduced myself. Little did I know how well-informed she was about church news and my latest stewardship message (in which I'd said we should not rely on fundraisers to pay church operating expenses).

Upon hearing my name, she rose up in righteous indignation and declared, "I've heard of you! You don't believe in fundraisers. How's the church going to stay open! I don't want to talk to you!"

Fearing that my being there a moment longer might kill her, I began to leave. As I passed the gray-haired lady in the next bed, she quietly said, "I'll talk to you." So I stopped to visit with her. She tried to console me with the knowledge that her roommate blasted a variety of people who came to visit.

While we talked, a couple came to see the lady by the window. She proceeded to tell them about that awful pastor who'd just been there, not realizing I hadn't left. After going on about the worthless wretch I was, she added, "But I hear his wife is nice." I guess I should have sent her.

That unpleasant encounter led to my meeting and visiting regularly with her roommate. Upon her release, she invited me to her home for a lunch of homemade soup with her and her little dog. Many pleasant conversations and a warm friendship developed.

Life consists of a number of these chance encounters. I've never been thrown out of a hospital room before or since that day, but that event led to a blessing for that roommate and for me. One door closes, another one opens they say—even if the door hits you on the backside while you're on the way out!

Another time, I went to visit a church member in the hospital and wound up befriending the roommate. The roommate's neighbor was at his bedside. Lengthy theological discussions filled our time together. The neighbor would debate and question numerous things. The patient watched us as one would watch a tennis match.

During the next year or so, I'd be visiting a church member in the hospital and to my surprise this neighbor woman would be in the next room. This time it was her chronically ill husband in the bed. A month or so later, I'd drop by a hospital patient's room, and there she and her husband would be, either right next door or at least on that hall. These encounters led to her calling me to discuss the Bible and my visiting them at their apartment. When he died, she asked me to conduct his funeral.

I'd thought that they only had one adult son. But at the funeral, I met seven adult children. Neither she nor her husband had mentioned them. There was obvious bitterness and division. Who caused what I do not know. But I was there, and perhaps it was because I had the message they needed to hear. At the graveside service, I spoke about mortality and the inevitability of a near future date when they would be back at that graveside. I admonished them to pursue forgiveness and reconciliation while there was still time.

Unless those "chance" encounters had happened and our relationship, forced by timing and circumstance, had not grown and deepened, they may not have heard that message. None of the family had a church or a pastor. As Mordecai said to Queen Esther of her longshot good fortune of being the queen of Persia, perhaps I was crossing paths with that couple "for such a time as this" (Esther 4:14).

I have also had chance encounters in which someone crossed my path at the right time for my sake. I imagine our sovereign God looking from heaven down upon earth, watching the lives of people as they live and move about. How often has He interceded and made my path cross with that of another at just the right time?

While two hundred miles from home on a bicycling trip through Roanoke, Virginia, I'd just used my last spare tube and tire. I needed a bike shop. As I mounted my bike, alongside of me a racing bike with its rider in full garb pulled up—just in time to give me directions.

While I was researching the life of nineteenth-century circuit rider Robert Sheffey, a man struck up a conversation as I ate lunch in a Radford, Virginia, restaurant. Turned out that he happened to know the late author of the book I'd been using to explore Mr. Sheffey's travels.

When I chose a church to attend in Sheffey's boyhood hometown of Abingdon, I happened to meet Mrs. Pat Sheffey, who likewise had researched the man's life. She had married one of his great-grandsons. She was one of the wisest of people and a dear friend for many years.

Chance meeting? Someone has said that a coincidence is when God acts anonymously.

Look at the faces of the people you pass every day. Each one has a story, is on a journey, and is a walking library of experiences and knowledge. Through the most unlikely encounters, however brief, God may be helping you more than you know—yet.

> Behold, God is my helper; the Lord is with those who uphold
> my life. (Psalm 54:4)

The Used-to-Bes and the Gonna-Bes

You scan the radio and hit upon a song that takes you back in time. A good experience or a time of challenge, the song brings up pictures on your mind's view screen. The emotions of that time even begin to return. Sometimes that's good and comforting and even brings a smile to your face. Other times you recall this as background music that seemed to be playing everywhere as you drove to a job you despised or went to places where good memories turn painful now because that place, as it was, is gone, and so are the people who had made it special.

Change is the only thing on earth that is constant. The music of different time periods serves as mental index markers. My wife was amazed when we used to hear a song on the radio and I could usually recall the year it came out. These were songs from my days of working in restaurants and then the twelve-hour shifts in the health club. The radio played all day. I used to call it "spar music." On the eastside of Baltimore I worked in a fitness center where the members called the spa, the "spar." One guy actually wrote his dues check out to "Holiday Spar."

Well, so what?

As we rack up mileage, we start getting into conversations at parties or at family gatherings or at cookouts with old friends. We eventually talk about what used to be. The older you get, the longer the list of "used-to-bes" gets to be. The list breaks into chapters. A move, a death, a change in health or career usually marks the end of what used to be. Then you'd look ahead toward what's gonna be. There would be new routines, new environment, new friends, new bills to pay, etc.

Even if you were looking forward to what's gonna be, you'd still look back over your shoulder and remember, "A year ago today I was doing such and such." It used to be we did this, but now we're gonna be doing this other thing.

Life constantly moves forward. There is no reverse gear. Trouble comes to us when we try to stop moving. Life doesn't have a "pause" button so you can run to the bathroom or get some popcorn or fix your hair. Nope, it keeps going, and you have to go with it as is. That's why in the Bible life is called a *walk*.

> We walk by faith, not by sight. (2 Corinthians 5:7)

That's tough to do because what comes into our sight can make faith tough to walk by.

> Faith is the substance of things hoped for, the evidence of things unseen. (Hebrews 11:1)

So you can't really *see* the substance of faith, but a lot of things you have seen seems to defy faith. So going forward with what is "gonna be" makes what used to be hard to let go. And because you can't throw it into reverse and go back, going forward is almost unthinkable. But *forward* is the only direction life goes. God gives us some comfort in the Scripture, a perspective from which we can scope out all of life (past, present, and future). Some say that things happen for a reason. I disagree. God takes what happens, the tragedies, our mistakes and failures, disappointments and betrayals, the hurt we've both endured and caused others, and He redeems it. He gives it a reason, using the broken pieces to mold together a new thing for a new day.

> And we know that all things work together for good to those who love God, to those who are called according to His purpose. (Romans 8:28)

From that perspective as well as the fact that Jesus Christ is "the same yesterday, today and forever" (Hebrews 13:8), we can keep moving forward. Look at the chapters of life, those written and yet-to-be written, this way: *gonna-bes are used-to-bes that haven't happened yet.* Everything eventually becomes "used to be."

Maybe we could appreciate special people and life's experiences now, and be more accepting of its passing when it does, if we would live in the past now. People who live in the past after it has become the past are trying to go back—an impossible feat. Thus their good memories of what used to be has become a dark cloud over what's gonna be—and they have neither; can't go back, won't go forward.

Every year I take a long bicycling trip for about a week. I give thanks to God for this one last trip, appreciating every day I can do it. It may be the last one. Anything can happen—something is gonna be, so I'm thankful for what is.

Gonna-bes are used-to-bes that haven't happened yet. So embrace the moment you have while you have it.

Training on Loving Life

Two mornings per week, I take a forty-five-minute "spin class," an aerobics class that is done entirely on stationary bicycles. The instructor is up front, on a bike, barking out orders to shift the resistance to higher or lower levels—to stand and "climb the hill" or sit and spin our legs in a fifteen-second sprint. The good, experienced instructor knows his/her class, how far and how hard to push them, and when to back off for rest intervals.

One instructor was an upbeat, muscular, fifty-something man who picked a wide variety of music and encouraged his sweating students to "challenge yourself!" Sometimes after a particular set of climbs and sprints, he would smile and say, "You are looking strong. You are *loving life!*" A lot of us did not feel that way, but it was good to hear the leader set the standard and say, "Hey, you are doing okay, keep it up." Occasionally, our instructor would call on each member of the class, in the final twenty minutes of class, to take one minute and lead the group. A variety of styles resulted, and it was unpredictable how hard or easy that minute would be, depending on the sadistic nature of the student. The experienced leader was testing us to see who could replace him in the near future.

Within a few months, one of my classmates moved from cycling beside me to being the instructor. He had allergies and some lung capacity difficulties. Being a student was challenging enough, but when he had to spin and yell out the instructions and breathe, he struggled. Sometimes we got longer rest intervals because *he* needed it. However, there is something about the responsibility of leadership that empowers one to gain a new level of strength. Over time I observed his lung capacity improving, his need for a lengthy rest interval gone, and a heightened proficiency at yelling instructions while maintaining his own pace. We had been taking this class together for over a year, but now that he was teaching it, he had improved markedly in just a month. I saw in this a spiritual application.

The writer to the Hebrews cuts short his exposition on the high priesthood of Jesus Christ because they had become "dull of hearing" (Hebrews 5:11). They were unable to comprehend these deeper truths because they were not growing spiritually. Over time they had slumped into a rut of complacent immaturity.

> For though by this time you ought to be teachers, you need someone to teach you again the first principles of the oracles of God; and you have come to need milk and not solid food. For everyone who partakes only of milk is unskilled in the word of righteousness, for he is a babe. (Hebrews 5:12–13 NKJV)

Even the most skilled athletes or craftsmen, or anyone with special training, regresses without regular practice. Skills are sharpened and improved by continuously challenging them to reach a high standard of proficiency.

If you are not one to talk about or share your faith with someone who needs to know it, you will eventually lose your grasp of it yourself. Usually it will be a child who will ask a simple yet profound question about God, and you will be stumped. In that moment of futility, as you grasp for knowledge you once had, you will realize you are "out of shape"; you have become immature. As the writer admonishes us, "Solid food belongs to those who are of full age, that is, those who by reason of use have their senses exercised to discern both good and evil" (Hebrews 5:14 NKJV).

The Scripture tells us that if you are not actively "working out" (Philippians 2:12b) your faith and seeking to grow in what you know, you will lose what you had. Someone will have to "teach you again the first principles." The unskilled in the Word cannot receive the deeper insights nor grow to their full potential in faith because they are not handling, practicing, and working with what they have.

The command Jesus gave to all of His disciples is to go and make disciples, teaching them. (Matthew 28:20). Every one of us should have such an understanding of our faith that we could explain it. We are commanded to "work out" and mature in our knowledge of the Lord. (See 1 Peter 3:15; 2 Timothy 3:16–17.) "Challenge yourself! You are looking strong. You are loving life!" Yes, it's work. It will require discipline, but it feels so good when you are finally strong enough to "take that hill," and then with confidence to lead others to follow your example.

Jesus promised His followers an abundant life (John 10:10). Isn't it true that you work at the things you love? How much more would your love for God grow if you worked a little more on really knowing Him?

God Understands

The instructor jumps onto a stationary bike in front of the class, fast-paced music kicks in, and off we go. This is the typical spin class I have been part of for years. This class has pushed me to improve my lung capacity—a tough challenge. I pace myself with the instructors. I hear their directions, but I *follow their actions.*

It's grueling as we work through numerous climbs, standing runs, and sprints for about forty-five minutes. The results of this self-disciplined suffering far exceed the relatively brief time on the bike, although it doesn't seem that way at the time.

One class I'd taken became so popular that the instructor had to give up his bike to a class member and lead from the floor. I never liked that, because then he no longer was suffering with the rest of us. If I start wearing out, it helps to know he feels my pain. There is something to be said for the leader who suffers with the troops. He (or she) has been where you are. Thus, the good leader knows better than you how far you can go, even when you're ready to give up.

Perhaps you need this perspective on your current trial; for you it's been sort of a workout that will never end, grueling and painful. Does it help to know that God understands *by personal experience?*

> Seeing then that we have a great High Priest who has passed through the heavens, Jesus the Son of God, let us hold fast our confession. For we do not have a High Priest who cannot sympathize with our weaknesses, but was in all points tempted as we are, yet without sin. (Hebrews 4:14–15 NKJV).

So what does that do for you? Jesus is both fully God and has lived on earth, fully human. He was able to live a perfect life, never falling to the power and temptations of sin because His human self was under the full control of God's Spirit.

> For in Him dwells all the fullness of the Godhead bodily. (Colossians 2:9 NKJV)

We have Jesus Christ as the example of the holy life. A human being completely submitted to the authority and power of God can turn from sin and live unto God. It is not, of course, the goodness of humanity that makes that possible—for there is no goodness in the heart of man (Jeremiah 17:9) or in human nature (Romans 3:10–23). But God has made a way for you.

The end result of sin is death (Romans 6:23), and Christ as our great High Priest has offered the perfect sacrifice of Himself—the substitute who died in our place (Isaiah 53:4–12, Hebrews 9:12–14)—so that atonement has been made. What has stood between us and God has been taken out of the way. God does understand your burdens, the painful memories, the consequences you bear today because of yesterday's choices; all these are before the Lord who knows where you've been and what has happened. And so the Scripture assures you: in Jesus, God has experienced *personally* how tough life can be, and He is aware of those intense challenges that cause stumbling and those that invite even the believer to stray.

> Let us therefore come boldly to the throne of grace, that we may obtain mercy and find grace to help in time of need. (Hebrews 4:16 NKJV)

There is help. There is grace. Why do we allow pride to convince us we can take it, that "I've got it under control"?

"Come boldly," He says. What boldness there must be in true humility. Have you ever thought of that?

It takes a determined, gutsy humility to bow before God and admit. "I can't do this." He already knows. He's just been waiting for you to finally recognize it yourself.

Call upon Me in the day of trouble; I will deliver you, and you shall glorify Me. (Psalm 50:15 NKJV)

We don't glorify God by how good we can be; we glorify God by letting Him make us into what, in our own power, we could never be. A lot of things are impossible for you, but all things are possible with God (Matthew 19:26). Pace yourself; hear His words, but follow His example (1 Peter 2:19–25).

Run through Your Agony

In the Bible, living by faith has been described as a race.

> The time of my departure has come. I have fought the good fight, I have run the race, I have kept the faith. (2 Timothy 4:5–7)

> Do you not know that those who run in a race all run, but one receives the prize? (1 Corinthians 9:24)

> You ran well, who hindered you? (Galatians 5:7)

> Let us lay aside every weight, and the sin which so easily ensnares us, and let us run the race that is set before us. (Hebrews 12:1b)

The word *race* is a good description of what it is to live the Christian life, to live according to the godly, scriptural standards of our faith in Christ. The word is translated from the term *agone*, from which we get the word *agony*.

Anyone who has ever run, bicycled, or done any other kind of competitive event that requires endurance knows what agony is all about in the agone—the race. We are simultaneously competing against two opponents. The first opponent is our immediate adversary in the race. We are striving to stay ahead and defeat the one who is striving just as hard to defeat us.

The other opponent is the exhaustion and pain that is screaming at our brains as we give it our all. In the race, the muscles are aching, perhaps knotting up. The lungs are straining for air, the throat is dry, and the limits of our strength and capacity are being pressed hard. The inner voice says, "I'm getting tired. It hurts. I want to stop. I cannot wait till this is over!"

Agony is the dual struggle against the strength of your adversary and the weakness of yourself. When I was about twelve, I raced my single-speed Sears bicycle on a course around the inner harbor of Baltimore. I was competing against other kids, and some of them had five-speed bikes. My grandmother tied my number to my back by wrapping the string around and knotting it in front.

I made good time against the other kids, and as I pumped up the hill toward the finish line, a very determined girl was right behind me. I would not let a girl beat me. Twelve-year-old boys cannot suffer such disgrace. As I gave my all to keep ahead of her, my lungs were screaming for air and I was getting lightheaded. My grandmother had tied the string too tight. I was in agony! I longed to stop, but I kept pedaling, one stroke at a time.

I finally crossed the line, won the race, and collapsed by a tree. I had pressed on through the agony, defeating a strong opponent and conquering my own inner desires to give up and quit. The Christian life is like that. It is a race. It is sometimes sheer agony.

In life you will have numerous opponents striving against you, attempting to ruin your walk with the Lord: pride, the lust of the eyes, the temptation to compromise and play life the world's way, and the desires that are part of a wealthy, materialistic culture. In the church we have opponents too: heretics in the pulpits and Sunday schools, gossips and backbiters in the pews, and leaders whose good intentions may actually be a device of Satan to lead us astray.

Opponents are strong and well trained, and they, like any worthy opponent, have studied our weak spots. In a race you guard your vulnerabilities, and you never take your strengths for granted.

The other opponent is the voice within. Struggling to stay faithful and to say no to temptations requires energy and tenacity. Often you will get weary. Exhaustion can make you ache for relief. It is tempting to give up and to give in. Living in the world and not of it, as Jesus calls us to do, is not an easy call. It is agony. The finish line is something a long way off, and the rewards for staying in the race and running strong and with perseverance can be few and far between. But we must run on. We must run through the agony.

The apostle Paul writes from a cold, dark horrible prison:

> ...one thing I do, forgetting those things which are behind and reaching toward those things which are ahead, I press toward the goal for the prize of the upward call of God in Christ Jesus. (Philippians 3:13–14)

How do we do that? How do we run the race with perseverance and strain toward what is ahead? The writer of Hebrews tells us the following:

> Let us run with endurance the race that is set before us, looking unto Jesus, the author (originator) and finisher of our faith, who for the joy that was set before Him endured the cross, despising the shame, and has sat down at the right hand of the throne of God. (Hebrews 12:1b–2)

The joy set before Him was Easter morning, the defeat of the power of death, the salvation of the souls of all who would believe in and receive Him. Nothing we have gone through is equal to the suffering He endured. But the victory He achieved is ours to live in now.

> For consider Him (Jesus) who endured such hostility from sinners against Himself, lest you become weary and discouraged in your souls. You have not yet resisted to blood shed striving against sin. (Hebrews 12:3–4)

The race that is the Christian life is never easy. If you are truly striving to live and walk closer to Jesus, your opponents in the world will be many and varied. The course will sometimes be painfully exhausting, to the point that you will consider quitting. Run through it! Carry these words as you go: "I can do all things through Him who strengthens me" (Philippians 4:13).

The Letter from Home

I love old photos and letters written by people from long ago. A visit to Monticello in Virginia to see the writings of Thomas Jefferson and walk the floors he had walked is fascinating. All of these historical things are like letters or messages from people of the past to us. My bicycle explorations through Virginia have taught me more about some of our presidents and the way things were in our nation's earlier days than any of my school textbooks. When I go to the source, I get the message from the source.

Our Bible is a collection of sixty-six messages, or books, from the Source of the truth. We call it the Word of God. In some churches, people stand when the gospel is read. In others, they stand for all Scripture readings. Various traditions have various ways of showing respect and reverence, and of identifying this book as the Word of God. But yet, when the Scriptures are read, few open their Bibles to follow along. People used to bring their Bibles to church. (In the nineteenth century, they carried their own hymnals, too.) Some still do bring their own Bibles, but in many churches, if not most, they are a minority. We say it is the Word of God, but we behave as if it's not. Perhaps we need to reconsider our own perspective on this book.

Let's say you are far from home—thousands of miles. For years you have not seen a loved one from your own hometown. Once in a great while a letter arrives, and that's the only contact you have with your family or that special someone. All you have of them is a handful of letters. Would you treasure them? Yes. Would you read them again and again, almost as if you would like to crawl into the page? Yes. Why are these few letters so special? They are a contact point.

The point of a pen that touched the paper was held in the hand you have longed to touch. And that hand was only several inches away from the heart or face of the one you miss and so want to see. And while that letter was being written, that piece of paper was surrounded by all the things of home. And it was folded by the hand of the one who wrote it. You want to be there. And that page and that ink was from there. And if you traced it back—from the paper, to the ink, to the pen, to the hand that held it, to the one holding the pen—that's as close as you can get to where you want to be.

The Bible is a letter from God. Getting into His Word is to seek the hand of the Writer, to want in your heart to be home. The gospel says this:

> In the beginning was the Word, and the Word was with God, and the Word was God. He was in the beginning with God. All things were made through Him, and without Him nothing was made that was made. In Him was life, and the life was the light of all men … And the Word became Flesh and dwelt among us. (John 1:1–4, 14a).

He came here personally so that we might find the way home. All of the Word of God, the Bible, His letter to us, points to Jesus Christ. And though we will be here on earth far away, and perhaps for quite some time from our true home, we have this letter.

Some people don't read it because they claim they can't understand it. In the conventional sense of understanding, they are right. It's only in knowing the Writer that we can come to understand the contents of His letter. If you really want to know Him, He will help you read it.

I once read a true story about a slave woman who believed in God and wanted to read the Bible. In those days, slaves were not taught to read, but God somehow made it possible that, though she was illiterate all her life, she could read and understand the Bible. The details of this account escape me, but the truth is clear: with God all things are possible. And our God went as far as dying on a cross to help us find Him. He helped a slave to read His Word. And He will help you … if you really want to know (see Acts 17:27). It's your move.

Trophies and Their Stories

What do your trophies mean to you? What comes to mind when you take a long look at each one? My Little League sports trophies, the two I won in oratorical contests, and even my citizenship trophy from high school are gone. They had become clutter, and finally I disposed of them.

But one small trophy remains on my desk at home; it was my first. A marble block with a gold plastic cyclist mounted on top; first place for a bike race I won when I was nine years old. It was at Federal Hill in South Baltimore, on the circular drive that now is covered over for a playground. In that park, twenty years after that milestone race, I proposed to Marcella. And then one day, that bicycle was proudly ridden by our eleven-year-old daughter, Elizabeth. What a story it tells.

The trophy takes me back to the Christmas morning when I saw that "big" gold bicycle with the shiny chrome fenders and steel training wheels sitting in front of the tree. It was a Sears Roebuck, single speed with twenty-four-inch wheels and white wall tires. I was almost seven years old, probably eight, when Dad took off the training wheels and coached me in the back alley. I only fell once. My dad had imparted to me a skill that (forty-plus years later) would take me on a twenty-one-speed bicycle, to Mississippi.

That first evening, just getting me to negotiate the alley from one end to the other was a victory. Then there would be the race, the trophy, and other adventures. I mastered that gold steed in riding and caring for it. Dad helped me with my first flat and other repairs. My dad could fix anything, but there came a time in my adult years when I brought house and car problems to him, but he brought bicycles to me. In that, I think my dad taught me discipleship. He was wise in many things, but once he introduced me to the bicycle, he encouraged me to become the wise one. For him, a bicycle was a toy; he helped me learn how to play with it and take care of it. But being a city boy who longed to be in the country, that bike for me was a ticket to freedom, adventure, and discovery. Like a cowboy and his horse, Roy Rogers with Trigger, there I was with my bike. It was no mere toy. Learning its nuances and maintenance needs took more focused attention, several bloody knuckles, greasy hands, and frustrating trial and error.

When I look at that humble little trophy, it means more to me now than it did when I was nine.

It's funny, but I don't remember the race. I do remember Dad teaching me in the back alley to ride. I recall falling as I turned around. I recall times when we worked on it together. So the trophy wasn't about winning the race. It represents how my father and I invested time in making me proficient enough to enter the race. If he was alive today, I think I would admit that the trophy belongs to him. He, however, would not have considered his contribution to be a big deal.

So the trophy also reminds me of my daughter riding that old gold bike. Though she received a new pink bicycle with flower designs and a handlebar basket, she chooses to ride the heavier old boy's bike. Over the decades, I have refurbished it and kept it roadworthy. I told her when she was six that someday she'd be riding that "big" gold bike. And then some years later she did—doing tricks, riding for miles, mastering it as if it had always been her own. When she rides it, I vicariously ride it again through her. I know what she's experiencing.

When I see that trophy, I recall the time and coaching my dad gave me. I try to carry that investment forward to my girls. What my own father probably saw as "no big deal" is actually bigger than he could ever have known. When he and Mom picked out that bike at Sears in 1966, they could never have known that one day their granddaughter would love that bike and make it her own.

Trophies are like memorials. While celebrating an achievement, they help us remember all that went into and led up to that victory.

Once Joshua led the Israelites through the parted Jordan River into the Promised Land, they built a memorial of twelve stones, so that when later generations asked, "What do these stones mean?" the story was told of how God dried up the Jordan just as He did the Red Sea. Then "all the peoples of the earth (will) know the hand of the Lord, that it is mighty" (Joshua 4:19–24).

Look at your trophies and awards. Ask, "What does this *mean?*" Winning the prize is not just about being better than the competitors. It's also about being better than *you* were before; and fully appreciating how and with whom you came into that race (or game). And … why does this matter to you now?

Ponderings of the Pedaling Pastor

Every summer I explore a part of the country on my bicycle. I go for about a week on my own; yet I'm never alone. It's my best time for prayer, reflection, and insight.

In 2012 we visited family in Indianapolis, Indiana. As my wife and daughters drove back home by car, I headed back on my bike. I wanted to explore the National Road (Route 40) and travel the route, for the most part, that the early pioneers took to settle this great land. I'd like to share some highlights from my seven-day journey.

Day 1

Leaving our hotel under the stars at 5:20 a.m. I picked up Route 40 east. Quiet, dark streets led me out of eastern Indianapolis into open country. It was flat and easy going. The air was humid but cool. The sun rose over brown lawns and fields of wilted, dried-up crops. The drought has been severe.

Thirty miles out, it was 7:15 a.m. as I stopped at quaint and quiet Knightstown. I was drawn to a beautifully landscaped median on a wide side street. It led to an elaborate and classy veterans' memorial in a quiet garden. At the back was a granite wall with a quote from George Washington: "The willingness with which our young people are likely to serve in any war, no matter how justified, shall be directly proportional to how they perceive the Veterans of earlier wars were treated and appreciated by their nation."

The most lavish decoration in many of the towns is their Veterans Memorial. Freedom is never free. Does my generation appreciate this truth as much as our predecessors? Rudyard Kipling's words are profound: "God and soldier we adore In times of danger and before. Danger past and all things righted, God is forgotten, the soldier slighted." An eighty-two-year-old gentleman, Mervin Kilmer, greeted me and told me that the movie *Hoosiers* had been filmed there—a proud claim to fame for Knightstown, Indiana. He invited me to join him for breakfast with friends at the local donut shop/grill. I had two big pancakes, enjoying my time in their world. These four men and one woman meet weekly for breakfast and to share life. I have noticed as I pass through countless villages and towns that small groups of seniors gather in local eateries to discuss the issues of the day. As Mervin, a retired Quaker pastor, explained, the politicians ought to be talking to them. They've already worked out the answers to the world's problems over breakfast. No doubt the collective wisdom of these little restaurant groups across the nation are an untapped resource of knowledge and experience. Pay a consultant a huge fee or have a breakfast meeting with folks like these? Perhaps the answers are more easily found than we realize.

Give instruction to a wise man, and he will be still wiser; teach
a just man, and he will increase in learning. (Proverbs 9:9)

It got very hot as I pressed on into Richmond and across the Ohio
line. A statue of the Madonna of the Trail (one of several along the
National Pike) stands as a testament to the many women who held a
child in one arm and a rifle in the other as they raised their families
in the harshest of conditions. When we think we have things rough,
remember these early pioneers who had only their hopes and dreams up
ahead and the arduous task of just surviving one day at a time.

At the ninety-two-mile mark, I rested at a Sunoco convenience
store. One customer took a look at my sweaty, dirty appearance and
proudly suggested that I enter the Tough Mudder event in Mayfield,
Kentucky (www.toughmudder.com). He planned on doing it, describing
an incredible obstacle course that sounds like a Special Forces boot
camp odyssey. Looking at my bike, he seemed to be implying that
if I was crazy enough to do this, I would love to do that. Was that a
compliment?

At Vandalia, Ohio (north of Dayton), my day was done at 2:10 p.m.
with 104 miles completed. I had a late lunch at the KFC near my hotel
stop. Two-for-one pot pie; the extra would be my supper. Good deal.
Then another patron came in to buy a quick lunch. The clerk sold
him on the pot pie deal. He looked over at me, and having no need for
the free one, he gave it to me. So supper was free that night. You just
never know who you will meet or what blessings you may receive along
the way.

It would take me two more days to get across Ohio on the historic
National Road. As I pedaled along, I reflected on what these journeys
must have been like two centuries ago. It had been George Washington's
vision that a road be cut westward into the Ohio Country, as it was
called. It was the western wilderness and part of the British Colony
of Virginia. One did not go *to* Ohio; one went *into* Ohio. It was a
densely forested, dangerous region. In fact, as I later learned, the city
of Wheeling, West Virginia, which sits on the Ohio line, was named
for a murder. The Indian term translated "weeling" means "head." So
Wheeling was actually "Murdering Town," because the head of some

unfortunate European traveler was put on a stake on the bank of the Ohio River as a warning by the Indians. Sort of a primitive, "Do Not Enter" sign.

Along this road, the boots and wagon wheels of thousands of unnamed pioneers preceded me. I crossed paths with George Washington, Lewis and Clark, the French army, and numerous Native American tribes.

At the end of the day, I was drenched in sweat, tired, and dirty. I had a hot bath, a good meal, and a soft bed in a safe place. It wasn't like that for a traveler two hundred years ago. Yet it is because of their courage, and vision, and God's grace, that I can safely make this trip as others have before me.

Ponder the blessings.

> Blessed is the nation whose God is the Lord, the people He has chosen as His own inheritance. (Psalm 33:12)

Day 2—Tuesday, 6:30 a.m.

A warm sunrise departure from Vandalia, Ohio, became a clear, very hot day on the National Road. Leaving the urban/suburban surroundings, the still relatively flat road led me through a variety of scenery. Long stretches of country road would open to dual highways lined with cornfields and a few houses here and there. Lawns and fields were green, as if heaven had turned on the faucet east of the Indiana/Ohio border.

In Springfield, an old town that had served the needs of generations of westbound travelers on this road, remnants of former times of growth stand idle among the newer high rises and urban beautification projects. The ornate architecture of some of these very old buildings would be costly to duplicate. There seems to be a certain pride of craftsmanship and artistic detail from past generations that one rarely sees today. Clean, practical, and cost-effective is the objective in modern building. In Springfield, these old beautiful dinosaurs stand amid the clean lines of modern architecture and one has to wonder: Are we missing something? Buildings have character, don't you think? They tell a story, sometimes several stories.

The block-long City Building was built in 1890 for $250,000. A meat, fish, and produce market and other vendors had occupied the first floor. The second and third floors housed city offices, the Police Department, the City Council Chambers, and City Hall, which doubled as an opera house. If walls could talk, imagine what they could tell …

I wondered what the story was as I passed through a stately neighborhood of older homes, many with the "gingerbread" style of trim and wooden porches. Within a six-block stretch, I passed *four* funeral homes. There were also several large church buildings. Scripture says that at the coming of the Lord Jesus, He will descend from heaven with a shout …

> And the dead in Christ will rise first. Then we who are alive and remain will be caught up together with them … to meet the Lord in the air. (1 Thessalonians 4:16–17)

Perhaps a lot of these folks will be from Springfield, Ohio.

At the sixty-two-mile mark, I came upon a marker. The little village of Franklinton was founded in the "unbroken wilderness" in 1797 by Lucas Sullivant and a company of twenty men. He established the court, the church, and the school and built the first bridge across the Scioto River. Today this is the west side of Columbus. The marker identified where Sullivant's cabin had stood.

The downtown is modern and beautiful. The promenade along the east bank of the river has gardens and fountains and swinging benches for relaxing in the shade. As I ventured about downtown, I felt drawn to go back to a deli I had passed. Over lunch, the clerk advised me to alter my route to pick up Route 40 from a safer street. I did that and found a quiet, tree-lined street, which led to a section of fine shops and calm traffic. Reminded me of Chevy Chase or Georgetown, Maryland.

I looked for the hotel on Brice Road, ready to stop. Neither left nor right onto the road seemed correct from what I could see. So I pressed on two more miles. At the convenience store, I asked directions. They advised me to go back; the hotels were there, they said. But I have this thing about backtracking. (It's probably spelled P-R-I-D-E.) I was tempted to press on eastward; certainly there will be something. More than one person said it was not likely.

As I wasted twenty minutes debating, time was running late. I sucked up the "P" word, and headed back. Realizing I'd just biked two extra miles, this would be two more. Tomorrow, I had to do it *again*. "Get over it," I said to my bike. (I certainly didn't want to hear me say it.) And sure enough, I turned on Brice, went farther beyond what I could see, and there it was: the Red Roof Inn.

For we walk by faith, not by sight. (2 Corinthians 5:7)

What had I done wrong before? I read the directions from my perspective on Route 40. The directions were written from the perspective of the interstate exit. Lesson? *Perspective is key to understanding.* Sometimes you're not getting the answer because you are reading things from where *you* are standing. It is quite likely that if the wisdom you seek is bigger than you, and in an unfamiliar place, your perspective is skewed. Often God will lead through the word of others. It's pride that resists receiving advice.

> Where there is no counsel, the people fall; but in the multitude of counselors there is safety. (Proverbs 11:14)

The next day, I rode over forty miles before I saw another hotel. (Ouch!)

Day 3—Wednesday

It was eighty degrees before sunrise, and as the red ball climbed in the sky, the day became oppressively hot and humid. The flat terrain heading eastbound out of Columbus allowed a fast pace and a form of air conditioning on the bicycle. The pressure of traffic in the morning rush hour kept me moving through the green lights and whizzing past some flickering objects I recognized, only after my wheels had rolled by them; it was money.

I rode over two quarters, one partially embedded in the asphalt. Later, a penny. Then a dime and some more pennies. After I had bypassed a total of eighty-one cents in less than twenty miles, I began stopping to pick up the coins. I counted about $1.14 just that day. I thought, *Here's the solution to the national debt crisis. It's lying in the streets! Pay the whole thing off with pocket change.* After all, this was literally "found money" on just one small portion of one major road. Sometimes the answers to our most vexing problems are just lying in our path waiting to be found.

The sign at Kirkersville United Methodist Church grabbed my attention. It says the pastor is Van Winkle (first name: Rip?). The words it bore proved prophetic by day's end: "God Promises a Safe Landing Not a Calm Passage."

My first major hill climb was at Eagles Nest, so named for a large granite rock at the top that bears carved images of a Conestoga wagon, an automobile, and the distances to Columbus (32 miles) and Cumberland, Maryland (220 miles). It marks the first major improvement to the National Road since it was built in 1825. The twenty-nine-mile section from Zanesville west to Hebron was paved with concrete. It was "experimental paving," jointly funded by the local, state, and federal governments.

The brick manufacturers in Zanesville protested against the federal government's insistence on concrete instead of brick. Concrete met the $16,000 per mile budget; brick did not. (So there *was* a time when the government could keep to a budget.)

Money seems to be the theme for the morning. At 10:25, I came upon the N. T. Gant house on the edge of Zanesville. Partially refurbished, this old brick home with wooden door and window frames displays Gant's name prominently in the glass over the front door.

He was born into slavery on a Virginia estate in 1821. In 1845, his master died and a provision in his will set Gant free. He came across the Ohio River to Zanesville, where he worked to buy a farm and build his house. He owned a salt lick and prosperous coal mine. This man who entered the world as someone's "property" worked hard, saved money, and acquired more than three hundred acres of his own property. When he died in 1905, he was a well-respected citizen and a self-made millionaire. Anyone who wants to blame their circumstances and say, "I can't," needs to check out Mr. Nelson T. Gant. Wow!

Another Ohio success story is former US Senator John Glenn. When I was a kid, I had a GI Joe "Friendship 7" space capsule, modeled after the one he flew in 1962 as the first man to orbit the earth. Then Lt. Col. John H. Glenn Jr. was born in New Concord, Ohio, the town just up the road from the Zane Grey-National Road Museum.

While touring that museum, the staff said that John and Annie Glenn would be at his New Concord boyhood home (now a museum). It was his ninety-first birthday, and a party was scheduled for 4:00 p.m.

I arrived at 4:00 p.m. and saw a crowd of all ages gathering at this ordinary, yet attractive single-family home with a front porch, gray siding, and white trim. The basement, ground-level entrance in back had a line through the gift shop area into the small meeting room that had memorabilia and historic photos and mementoes on the walls. First I was in the cake-walk line (for cake, ice cream, punch). I got quick shots with the digital camera, but Senator and Mrs. Glenn were at a table surrounded by crowds.

I escaped the mob, went outside, and considered the moment. Black clouds gathered above, and rumbling sounds were getting closer. Meanwhile, ninety-one-year-old astronaut and Senator John Glenn was a few yards from me, and that is not likely to happen again. So I plunged back in, bought postcards, and had my pen. Within twenty minutes, I had three autographs and a photo of myself alongside him. And I could tell the folks at home, "I went to John Glenn's birthday party."

The rumbling intensified. I rode hard out of New Concord toward my hotel stop in Cambridge. The sky burst open; sheets of rain, lightning, thunder. *Trouble.* Visibility dropped, cars pulled over. Now drenched, I had to press on to avoid hypothermia. In the midst of this dangerous situation, a Honda pulled alongside; the driver understood that no one could see me, so he followed me, flashers on, all the way to Cambridge (ten miles). He literally "had my back." The rain felt good; fear of lightning did not. But I was safe. The Honda man's timely appearance reminded me of Hebrews 13:2: "Do not forget to entertain strangers, for by so doing some have unwittingly entertained angels."

Was he an angel or just a conscientious man? Who knows? (Remember the sign at Kirkersville.) I was safely in Cambridge: seventy-two miles.

Over thirty-plus years of riding tens of thousands of miles by myself, I know this: I have never been alone.

Day 4—Thursday

I spent the night in Cambridge, Ohio, the 250-mile halfway point between Indianapolis and home. Little did I know how much harder the last half of this trip was going to be. I was back on Route 40 east by 7:45 a.m. and enjoying the cool morning air. Last night's thunderstorms added a refreshing feel to the breeze.

As the National Road occasionally merges with I-70, I had to detour south. Six miles out of Cambridge, I was turned right on Route 265, a back road that rolled through back country fields and little villages.

I saw to my right a paved path across a field. At an intersection, I turned onto it and followed it through the woods until I came upon a community with a pavilion, some historical markers, and a playground. It was the village of Lore. From here the Labor Train would deliver coal miners to their work sites. The repairmen who serviced the tracks were called "Gandy Dancers" because their tools were manufactured by the Gandy Company.

Other than the old photos and the markers that told the stories, there is no trace of what went on here. A whole industry had been the center of this town, and "progress" took away its reason to exist. Now, it's a beautiful bedroom community with fine homes and people who drive elsewhere to work. We have mixed feelings about progress, don't we?

We mourn what used to be as if its passing was a terrible thing. In a way that is true: endings are often sad. Nostalgia brings both a smile and a tear. But without change and growth, living things die. Few people like change, but where would we be without it? I was biking through what used to be densely undeveloped, dangerous wilderness. But centuries ago, some folks risked everything to leave what they had to discover what could be.

In fact, that's why today I know where Lore, Ohio, is and about Gandy Dancers. I got off the planned path.

Passing through Quaker City and Barnesville, then back onto the National Road, it was a roller coaster ride of hills—mostly *up*. My average pace was 13.5 miles per hour. I imagine that the wagon trains were a lot slower. Our ancestors must have been patient people.

All along the pike from Barnesville to St. Clairsville, I saw acres of campers, tents, and RVs for miles. There were vendors along the road, people setting up camp in neighborhood yards, and a lot of traffic. The "Jamboree in the Hills" was under way. It's the "Super Bowl of country music" where folks gather annually to hear great bands and singers.

Two centuries ago, similar gatherings of wagons and tents spread across the country. The camp meeting brought out folks to hear great preaching by Methodist, Baptists, Presbyterian and others all on the same platform. They say there's a lot of drinking and such at the jamboree. The same things happened at camp meetings too. Being spirit-filled has meant different things to different people.

Arriving in Wheeling, West Virginia, I discovered that all but the pricier hotels were full. Exhaustion overwhelmed good sense, and I settled for pricey. One night cost what I'd spent for the last three nights combined. I succumbed to a desire to treat myself. When I saw the fancy linens, nice furnishing, and quality facilities, I thought, *Wow, I could get used to this.* And then I realized that is what is wrong in corporate and government leadership. They *are* used to this. This is the norm, and it is their *entitlement*. I was very self-conscious, and that taught me.

I explore the history of our country to acquaint myself with the suffering and sacrifice that was the norm for those who settled this great land. I ache at the end of these hard rides. Today was sixty-two miles of mostly climbing. I want to remember how hard it was for those who came before us. We have it so easy today because it was so hard yesterday. Have we learned anything?

What sacrifices will we need to make today to smooth the way for tomorrow's America? Or are we too soft now?

Day 5—Friday

I awoke at 4:00 a.m. to the sound of rain outside. I bound everything in waterproof wrapping and had some quiet time with my Bible, preparing myself for the challenge awaiting me.

It was a cool, misty departure out of Wheeling, West Virginia—a town named from an Indian word meaning "head." Some called it "murdering town." In the eighteenth century, an unfortunate European had ventured into the Ohio wilderness. The Indians killed him, put his head on a stake, and planted it on the bank of the Ohio River—a graphic way of saying, "Don't even *think* of coming over here."

As I was heading east on Route 40, I considered the Wheeling story a fitting theme. The eastbound route was murder on both my bike and my body. As I climbed the long ascents, I was dodging holes and cracks in the road. Then on the downhill runs I was standing on the pedals to let the bike bounce under me. It jarred me with such force that my panniers (the "saddlebags" hanging on the rack over the rear wheel) would bounce forward against my heels. A few times, one bounced off onto the road.

I saw the "Old National Pike," veering right to West Alexandria, so I checked it out. More climbs, but no progress. It became gravel after two miles, resulting in wasted time and energy, forcing me to double back. I chalked it up as a little adventure and resumed the former course on Route 40. "Stay positive, be patient ..." Then I tried *Bike PA East* and got lost. My goal for lunch was Washington, and it took me there (I'm not sure how). I pushed on to Uniontown, climbing Van Voorhis Hill (1445 feet) at 1:00 p.m. I'd ridden forty-eight miles, but it felt like a lot more. Being overcast and humid made for an ugly day but a better ride. Clear and sunny is pretty but also pretty draining. The sun can suck the energy out of you.

By the time I got to Brownsville, a periodic rain had started. Stopping by an old toll house, I tried to imagine the wagons and horses going by. What hard, dusty work it was to travel. And if these paved roads were rough today, how much worse it must have been on dirt and mud back then.

I got to Uniontown at 3:00 p.m. with sixty-nine miles and over five and a half hours of riding time. The road was becoming more and more difficult as I got closer to home. My average pace this day was 12.5 miles per hour. The old word for patience, *long-suffering*, is fitting.

Strength and talent often are untapped resources if you don't have the patience to stick to the task.

A Reflection

I left a town this morning whose legacy began with a murder. Unbeknownst to me or anyone else, a twenty-four-year-old man was planning a massacre out west. While I was bicycling across the Pennsylvania countryside, two other cyclists in Colorado were taking a break and going to the movies tonight in Aurora.

My loved ones worry about my riding on open roads, because of "the nuts out there." Yet, for those two riders, the nut (gunman James Holmes) came to them, in a typically safe, secure place.

There is such a randomness to daily living. Simple decisions, innocent choices can change the course of your day—or your life. Because of the decisions others are making, the pathways may cross, and a mixture of circumstances collide. From this, new situations are born; sometimes old standbys fall or are changed forever.

At any time you may have an appointment with destiny. My weeklong exploration of the National Road has brought me insights and expanded my knowledge of history. It's a highlight, a good memory from my life's journey.

But for these two other adventure-seeking cyclists a couple of thousand miles west, they rode into a national tragedy, a personal nightmare in their journey. The whole nation stopped at Aurora, Colorado.

For five days I explored our nation's history, appreciating the sacrifices of prior generations who established this country and died for the cause of liberty. Perhaps this generation's role is not to die for our freedoms in some war. Our role is to *live* in freedom right here and now. Terrorists can't steal freedom. Its source is God, and we lose it by giving it away.

In the rich beauty of these United States, evil hijacks the rights that freedom affords to us all.

> Do not fret because of evildoers … For they shall soon be cut down like the grass, and wither as the green herb. Trust in the Lord, and do good; dwell in the land, and feed on His faithfulness. (Psalm 37:1a, 2–3)

Day 6—Saturday

Overnight rain left damp roads and a cool, humid morning as I headed east toward the Allegheny Mountains. Leaving Uniontown, Pennsylvania, at 7:45 a.m., I looked toward the horizon and saw a break in the trees at the very top of the distant ridge. There was a barely visible section of road and a building *way up there*. I thought about the westbound pioneers and said to myself, "Surely they would not bring the National Road up through there." But alas, my hopes were dashed. They did.

It was the hardest, longest climb of the week (at least until that afternoon). I would also be facing Winding Ridge Summit (2601 feet) and Negro Mountain (2875), and a few others I was too tired to stop and write down.

This first big climb was up to the Laurel Highlands overlook. The Summit Resort is the building I had seen in the distance from Uniontown. It was about five miles of straight up; by day's end I was pacing at barely eleven miles per hour. It was as psychologically challenging as it was physically daunting. I thought to myself, A *lazy person would not do this.* Some would say that neither would a sane person who owns a car.

I also considered this from the perspective of people in recovery. Breaking an addiction to drugs or alcohol is both psychologically and physically overwhelming—a long, hard climb out of a deep, dark hole.

When I was at the bottom of the Laurel Ridge climb, I felt a sense of dread. The task was so overwhelmingly *up*, with no view of the top or any sense of how long it would take. Fortunately, calm rationality kicked in, and it was just a fact; I had to do this to get to the other side of it. Easier said than done, yes. Motivated? Not really. Was there pain involved? Eventually and certainly. All kinds of negatives about the task before me flooded my mind in a matter of seconds. I think that people fighting addictions experience this kind of flood; recovery and sobriety is just too high a mountain to conquer under one's own power. And they are right. There's another Power that can only be accessed one pedal stroke (or one step) at a time.

> I can do all things through Christ who strengthens me. (Philippians 4:13)

From the top, at the overlook, I took a photo of the distant road I'd come from, *way at the bottom.* It can be done.

Coming upon Braddock Park, the old Braddock Road, and Fort Necessity I was immersed in rich history. If only these hills could speak and give witness to what was experienced along this very road.

It was in 1754, a twenty-two-year-old British army Lieutenant Colonel, George Washington, traveled through here from Cumberland. The French and British disputed over who had true claim on the Ohio Valley area. Washington and thirty-three British soldiers came upon a French encampment at Jumonville Glen (so named for the French commander killed there). Washington won the skirmish, then retreated to the Great Meadows where his men built a "fort of necessity." The French, with six hundred troops and one hundred Indians, surrounded it and rained bullets upon them for hours.

The following year, Major-General Edward Braddock marched through here to fight the French near present-day Pittsburgh. His thirty-five years of military experience was no match for the wilderness tactics of the enemy. He died of wounds sustained at the Battle of the Monongahela. Washington conducted the graveside service and ordered him buried in the middle of the Braddock Road to prevent anyone from mutilating his corpse.

I stood at Braddock's grave (discovered in 1804). I stood where a replica of Fort Necessity now stands. So many details, so many "what if" questions came to mind.

I'd learned that Washington's surprise skirmish with the French at Jumonville Glen lasted fifteen minutes and helped start the French and Indian War, which lasted seven years. I left Fort Necessity wondering why we never learned any of this in school. It was the first "world war," involving several European nations plus a confederacy of Indian nations over here.

By 6:00 p.m. I was rolling into downtown Cumberland. Sixty-six long miles, and I was ready to stop. The white obelisk marker at Wills Creek Bridge read "Cumberland-1." Here is where the National Road officially began. So many things began here.

There is something about retracing one's steps. When you misplace something, the best thing to do is retrace your steps till your memory can reconnect you to the last time you had it. Then you start walking forward through the pictures in your mind from that point up to the current moment. Somewhere along the path you see a clue, an insight. It's how we help our kids find lost shoes, books, toys, etc. It's also how we as a people have to find our lost heritage. Remember who gave us our freedom.

In Cumberland, the construction of the National Road began in 1811. For two hundred years this route westward has been here; no one could tell me how to get back to it from downtown.

> Thus says the Lord: Stand in the ways and see, and ask for the old paths where the good way is and walk in it; then you will find rest for your souls. (Jeremiah 6:16)

Day 7—Sunday

Downtown Cumberland, Maryland. No vehicles or people were out on the streets. Leaving the hotel at 7:45 a.m. under cloudy, gray skies, it was humid but cool. And between here and home, several major climbs were awaiting me.

I hoped to stop at a church along the way. It's part of the adventure on these long rides, to meet new people and see what God is doing in another community. I enjoy the fascinating experience of walking into a place I've never been before and by the end of my visit, feeling like I've known these folks for years. As Paul says,

> There is one body and one Spirit ... one Lord, one Faith, one baptism, one God and Father of all, who is above all, and through all, and in you all. (Ephesians 4:4–6)

The hotel clerk gave me computer-generated, GPS-style directions to Route 40, which included a basic map. No person to whom I'd spoken could tell the way. Amazing that people didn't know how to get to a road that had been there for two hundred years. What's worse is, even the hotel computer got it wrong. I was immediately misdirected by that printout, spending forty-five minutes riding around trying to find Route 40 east.

Finally as I passed Allegheny College, a landmark on the hotel's printout, I came to an intersection. I saw a gray-haired man parking his truck on the roadside, heading toward a yard sale in a parking lot. "Excuse me, sir," I asked, "Is this Route Forty?"

He shrugged and said, "I don't know," and walked away.

By then, I was annoyed. I had ridden several miles and climbed some steep hills, trying in vain to leave this town. It was like being in one of those science fiction/horror films, caught up in a parallel universe from which there was no escape. What was it with all these people (at least the ones I had met since last evening) that no one knew how to get out of there? But then I saw a gray head. My hopes were buoyed—ah-ha; an elder, a wise man! *Certainly he will know,* I think.

> The silver-haired head is a crown of glory, it is found in the way of righteousness … and the splendor of old men is their gray head. (Proverbs 16:31, 20:29b)

After encountering this man, I thought, *What do you mean, you don't know? You're an old guy—you're supposed to know!* (My apologies to seniors; I was only a few years away from qualifying for the senior's coffee at McDonald's myself.)

Some of us know a little about a lot and others know a lot about a little—but when you don't know much about where you are, *that's* a problem.

I climbed long, torturous hills, as the National Road blended into the interstate and Route 144 became the alternate. I climbed Fifteen Mile Creek Road and on up to Town Hill. It was beautiful and quiet. I was disappointed that I came upon no country church as I typically would along such roads. Only in Flintstone did I find a church, but the service time was too late.

I passed yard sales and people mowing. A relatively recent phenomenon, Sunday morning yard sales is a sad tradition our culture has adopted. Sunday mowing is also more common today. It's no wonder that "Sabbath" (meaning "to cease," to rest) is one of the Ten Commandments. God had to tell the Hebrew people, who had known only slavery for four centuries, to stop living like slaves. *"Rest, take a break. That's an order!"* Now, we insist on going back. How did folks in past generations have so much more time? Sunday was for rest.

Of course, there I was climbing mountains on a Sunday morning, but it wasn't "work." It was quiet, a time to just converse with God. Re-creation. That's the purpose of Sabbath.

When I picked up the paved rail trail at Pearre and rolled into Hancock, I stopped for lunch to "decompress." I was about to finish the final twenty miles and would be reentering my regularly scheduled life and the roles I play in it. I had *rested* for this past week, and it was good.

At 3:30 p.m., I rode into my driveway in Clear Spring, having ridden seventy-one miles that day. The grand total for the week, from Indianapolis to home, was 530 miles. It was 535 miles to get out there by car. Returning by bike was shorter and saved gas.

I was tired, but *refreshed*. Make sense? You just had to be there …

Truth Really Can Be Stranger than Fiction and More Reliable

Weird, strange, or otherwise peculiar events can happen in a person's life. Some people sound like they live a soap opera type of existence with incredible stories of love, loss, and amazingly complex accounts of this and that, and how it happened, when, and where.

My testimony is the Most Important *Point to Ponder*. It's the final chapter in this book (page 99). I had been reluctant to submit it for publication as I tried to read it from the perspective of someone who doesn't know me. I wondered what people might think. It is a strange story, a briefly summarized account of several significant portions of my faith journey. But as I think of it, these things are strange because we seldom hear such stories from people we know or from within the circles where we work, study, or play. It's tabloid-sounding stuff, or the stories you might read about in religious publications. But I submit that these accounts are more typical than most of us realize. Look out over a crowd of people in a mall, or in a park, or at a church, or in a stadium. There are numerous untold stories. People aren't sharing their personal experiences for the same reason I almost didn't: people will think I'm weird. (With me, it will simply confirm opinions already held by some.)

Yet what were we told to do in Scripture? If you have come to faith in Jesus Christ, you are not called to argue or convince people that what you believe is the truth. The simple command we received is this: be My witnesses. Don't argue. Don't be a defense attorney. God doesn't need that. Just tell what you have seen, heard, and experienced.

> But you shall receive power when the Holy Spirit has come
> upon you; and you shall be witnesses to Me in Jerusalem,
> and in all Judea and Samaria, and to the end of the earth.
> (Acts 1:8)

When the authorities and skeptics of their day tried to shut up the apostles' witness, Peter's response was calm, forthright, and honest.

> But Peter and John answered and said to them, "Whether it
> is right in the sight of God to listen to you more than to God,
> you judge. For we cannot but speak the things which we have
> seen and heard." (Acts 4:19–20)

Being thought of as weird, or radical, goes with the territory. Not that you have to be obnoxious; it's just that things of the Spirit are "foolishness" to those operating from a fleshly perspective (see 1 Corinthians 2:9–14).

I recall when I lived according to that worldview. Reading my article again from that perspective struck me. My story sounded weird, but I *had lived it.* The message had been clear to me: God would be there, guiding me through the rough uncertainties and uphill struggles of life. Not so much economic hardship but the absence of integrity in things one should be able to trust. Many reject the faith, and even God, because of such things. God would not let me turn away without first planting a seed of assurance for me to find later.

Church as an institution impressed me as irrelevant. Some of the biggest hypocrites I knew were Christians. I also met corrupt pastors. While working in management at a fitness center, I caught a pastor trying to sneak in without paying the guest fee. When I sat him down in my office, he proceeded to offer me a deal. Having been through professional sales training, I recognized that so had he, trying to "close me" on the value of giving him a free pass in exchange for "advertising" our club through his sermon illustrations.

Then one of the top radio preachers, from whom I'd learned so much, fell morally. Ironically he had authored books on love and marriage. Despite this and other similar experiences, God began calling me back to church and then into pastoral ministry. But why would I want to join this crowd?

While I was in seminary, I discovered that one of the pastors who had discipled me had also committed adultery over a decade before. Then I kept encountering preachers, professors, student pastors, and even bishops denying basic beliefs and core doctrines. But the call on my life kept at me. And I kept remembering God's assurance to me through that childhood dream. He's never let go of my right hand. Though others do fall, His steps have always held firm. As I have watched many who "claimed the name" embarrass that name and fall away, the message to me has been clear: *"Don't follow my followers; follow Me."*

I found that if I sincerely sought the truth and was willing to receive it, someone would cross my path with a well-timed word, an amazing testimony, a Scripture, a thought-provoking question. God was (and is) there. I have learned that my response to God cannot be determined or hindered by the behavior of others. Why do that? It's kind of dumb to not attend church because of the hypocrites. That's like refusing to see a doctor because his office is full of sick people. And am I so supremely "well"?

> For He Himself has said, "I will never leave you nor forsake you." (Hebrews 13:5b)

The Most Important Point to Ponder

Have you ever received a message *years* after it was sent; and yet, when it arrived it was right on time? This was my very first *point to ponder.*

At around age six, I saw myself in a dream with Jesus walking up a rocky incline. The scene was set, in color, inside a cave with perhaps a ten- to twelve-foot-high ceiling. I stumbled up the rocks with Him just behind and beside me, holding my right hand. He was sure-footed, and I was not. At the top of the incline was a great light. There was a throne within it. I could only see sandal-clad feet under the light, on a pavement that was like glass. Some twenty-six-plus years later, I found that these accounts describe very well what I saw:

> And they saw the God of Israel. And there was under His feet as it were a paved work of sapphire stone, and it was like the very heavens in its clarity. (Exodus 24:10)

> Also from the appearance of His waist and upward I saw, as it were, the color of amber with the appearance of fire all around within it; and from the appearance of His waist and downward I saw, as it were, the appearance of fire with brightness all around. Like the appearance of a rainbow in a cloud on a rainy day, so was the appearance of the brightness all around it. This was the appearance of the likeness of the glory of the Lord. (Ezekiel 1:27–28)

Aspects of the scene were emphasized in my sight: Christ holding my right hand, my stumbling as opposed to His surefootedness, the light at the top (this was God). I was given to know that an understanding would come to me in the future. Being just a boy, I thought little of it again. Then at age thirteen, with my dad in Vietnam, our church no help at all, and our new pastor failing my mom in pastoral care, I grew angry and thought to reject church and its teachings. Then as I entered my bedroom one day in 1973, the dream came instantly into my mind and I understood it. It was a message. Interesting that Psalm 73 summarizes my condition and God's assurance.

> Then my heart was grieved, and I was vexed in my mind. I was so foolish and ignorant; I was like a beast before You. Nevertheless I am continually with You; You hold me by the right hand. You will guide me with Your counsel, and afterward receive me to glory. (Psalm 73:21–24)

That dream coupled with church teachings I'd learned in Lutheran Sunday school helped me to not drift too far. Eventually, as I sought the truth, the Lord drew near to help me know Him. Television and radio ministries prompted me to search the Scriptures, to send for information, to question. A close friend witnessed to me; the integrity of her life and walk with Christ prompted me to earnestly seek the Lord, to know for sure that His Word is *His* Word.

While on a bike ride in 1984, I was talking to God, asking for some sign from Him that would clearly show me that the Bible and what my friend had witnessed to me about it was true. I encountered a man and woman along my route who had stopped me to ask, "Have you ever thought about what would happen to you after you die?" We sat in the backyard of their house to discuss whether the Bible is truly God's Word. The man described many details and things I'd never heard of before. When they bid me farewell, they invited me to stop back.

Within a year of that visit, I drove by the location of this encounter, looking for that house. It was not there. Not even an empty lot was there. It took a few years, but I finally realized that I had been given the requested sign.

> Do not forget to entertain strangers, for by so doing some have unwittingly entertained angels. (Hebrews 13:2)

Later as I struggled, honestly confessing that I did *not* want to go to church, the Lord clearly guided me to attend a local United Methodist church. I'd been invited by the pastor to give a talk. As I walked up the steps, the Holy Spirit spoke clearly in my spirit: "This is where you will go; this is where you will belong." And I did.

By then I knew that Jesus Christ died for my sins and rose from the dead. But to intimately know Jesus has been a growing experience. Only after I started attending church (Hebrews 10:25) did I really grow. How can one grow in the Lord while disobeying His Word?

Because I desired God's will for my life, I sought mentors to guide me. I finally accepted the call to pastoral ministry because of love for Him and His Word. My life is on the track it is on solely because of Christ and my desire to serve and to please Him.

Have you pondered the track you're on and how you got there?

About the Author

Dennis E. Whitmore was born and raised in Baltimore City, graduating from Towson University with a bachelor of science in business administration, with concentrations in management and marketing. Out of college, he pursued a career in health and fitness as a salesman, personal trainer, and manager in Baltimore-area health clubs for eight years. Through his experience in physical fitness training, the Lord taught him spiritual fitness. From there, he was called into ordained ministry. Graduating in 1995 from Wesley Theological Seminary in Washington, DC, he served in United Methodist churches for twelve years. In 2007, he received credentials through the Christian and Missionary Alliance. Currently he serves as senior pastor of Hilltop Christian Fellowship in Clear Spring, Maryland.

> Pastor Dennis's vision for ministry is the transformation of lives into the likeness of Christ through *Knowing the Lord, knowing the Word, and walking in both.*

> In Christ ... being built together for a dwelling place of God in the Spirit. (Ephesians 2:22 NKJV)

For over twenty years, Dennis has studied and taught the Bible as the primary authority and guidebook for life. His other ministries include:

- Walk Thru the Bible: associate instructor, teaching both the Old and New Testament "walk thru" live events.

- Radio Bible teacher on the twice-weekly "Points to Ponder" broadcast and cohost of the Sunday talk show, "Consider This," which explores contemporary issues through a biblical lens (WJEJ 1240 AM, Hagerstown, MD, www.wjejradio.com)
- Chaplain for the Clear Spring area FCA (Fellowship of Christian Athletes).
- Cofounder and vice president of the HUB NETwork (www.myhubnetwork.org), a 501c3 faith-based "network of relationships connecting regional, community resources to meet physical, emotional, and spiritual needs." Helping people Up to Be as God intended.
- Former president of the Baltimore Fellowship Foundation (a.k.a. Baltimore Breakfast Group), a monthly prayer breakfast ministry to the local business community.
- Speaker, seminar leader, and teacher for senior citizen and student groups, spiritual retreats and conferences, and local churches. An avid cyclist for over forty years, Dennis has used his bike to draw closer to the Lord and to serve others, earning him the title, "the Pedaling Pastor." For over thirty-three years, he's raised funds for the National Multiple Sclerosis Society's Bike MS Chesapeake Challenge, a 150-mile bike tour on Maryland's eastern shore.

After Katrina ravaged the Gulf states, Laurel, Maryland, adopted Laurel, Mississippi. In 2006, Dennis rode his bike 1,071 miles from Laurel to Laurel, "Riding for Roofs" to raise $10,000 in funds for home repairs for seniors.

Dennis resides in Clear Spring, Maryland, with his wife (since 1989), Marcella, and their daughters, Elizabeth (1999) and Joanna (2003).

**All photos taken with my own personal camera:
Canon Power Shot Sx210 Is**